Physical Characteris
Belgian Tervu. _...
(from the American Kennel Club breed standard)

Topline: Level, straight and firm from withers to croup. Croup medium long, sloping gradually to the base of the tail.

Body: Is square; the length measured from the point of shoulder to the point of the rump approximates the height.

Hindquarters: Legs powerful without heaviness, moving in the same pattern as the limbs of the forequarters. Thighs broad and heavily muscled. Stifles clearly defined, with upper shank at right angles to hip bones. Hocks moderately bent. Feet slightly elongated, toes curved close together, heavily padded, strong nails.

Tail: Strong at the base, the last vertebra to reach at least to the hock. At rest the dog holds it low, the tip bent back level with the hock. When in action, he may raise it to a point level with the topline giving it a slight curve, but not a hook.

Coat: The guard hairs of the coat must be long, close fitting, straight and abundant. The texture is of medium harshness. The undercoat is very dense. The hair is short on the head, outside the ears, and on the front part of the legs. Ornamentation consists of especially long and abundant hair around the neck, fringe of long hair down the back of the forearm; long and abundant hair trimming the breeches; long, heavy and abundant hair on the tail.

Abdomen: Moderately developed, neither tucked up nor paunchy. Ribs well sprung but flat on the sides. Loin section viewed from above is relatively short, broad and strong, but blending smoothly into the back.

Color: Body rich fawn to russet mahogany with black overlay. The coat is characteristically double pigmented wherein the tip of each fawn hair is blackened.

Size: The ideal male is 24 to 26 inches in height and female 22 to 24 inches in height measured at the withers.

Belgian
Tervuren

◇

By Dr. Robert Pollet

Edited by Muriel P. Lee

Contents

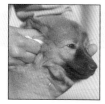

Training Your Belgian Tervuren 92

Begin with the basics of training the puppy and adult dog. Learn the principles of house-training the Belgian Tervuren, including the use of crates and basic scent instincts. Get started by introducing the pup to his collar and leash and progress to the basic commands. Find out about obedience classes and other activities.

Healthcare of Your Belgian Tervuren 117

By Lowell Ackerman DVM, DACVD
Become your dog's healthcare advocate and a well-educated canine keeper. Select a skilled and able veterinarian. Discuss pet insurance, vaccinations and infectious diseases, the neuter/spay decision and a sensible, effective plan for parasite control, including fleas, ticks and worms.

Showing Your Belgian Tervuren 144

Step into the center ring and find out about the world of showing pure-bred dogs. Here's how to get started in AKC shows, how they are organized and what's required for your dog to become a champion. Take a leap into the realms of obedience trials, agility, tracking and herding events.

KENNEL CLUB BOOKS® **BELGIAN TERVUREN**
ISBN: 1-59378-652-2

Copyright © 2007 • Kennel Club Books® • A Division of BowTie, Inc.
40 Broad Street, Freehold, NJ 07728 USA
Cover Design Patented: US 6,435,559 B2 • Printed in South Korea

Library of Congress Cataloging-in-Publication Data
Pollet, Robert, Dr.
Belgian tervuren / by Robert Pollet ; edited by Muriel P. Lee.
    p. cm.
ISBN 1-59378-652-2
1. Belgian tervuren. I. Lee, Muriel P. II. Title.
SF429.B42P65 2007
636.737--dc22
                    2007002446

10 9 8 7 6 5 4 3 2 1

Photography by Isabelle Français
with additional photographs by:

Ashbey Photography, Booth Photography, Paulette Braun, Carolina Biological Supply, Cott Photography, Tara Darling, Hodges Photography, Carol Ann Johnson, Bill Jonas, Dr. Dennis Kunkel, Tam C. Nguyen, Norton of Kent, Phototake, Dr. Robert Pollet, Jean Claude Revy, Susan and Lennah, Chuck Tatham, Karen Taylor and Riitta Tjörneryd.

Illustrations by Patricia Peters.

The publisher wishes to thank all of the owners whose dogs are illustrated in this book, including Diane Dykman, M. Edling, Maureen Foley, Frank and Charlene Mascuch, N. and S. Rose, Judith Lee Smith and Steve Sorensen.

With a combination of natural elegance, physical beauty, intelligence and a faithful temperament, the Belgian Tervuren has secured himself a place in the hearts of fanciers around the world and looks ahead to a bright future.

HISTORY OF THE

BELGIAN TERVUREN

Travel through Belgium and you will see the bustling cities of Antwerp and Brussels. When you travel through the countryside by car or train, you will also find beautiful farms and fertile, attractive fields. Imagine the Belgian shepherd dogs herding the cattle and sheep over these fields and you will have a picture-perfect scene. Belgium, of course, is the land of the four breeds of Belgian sheepdogs—the Groenendael, the Malinois, the Laekenois and the beautiful Tervuren.

The history of many breeds of dog is difficult to trace. In previous centuries very few, if any, records were kept of the dogs that were used for breeding. The best working dog at a particular task was bred to a similar animal who performed well at the same task. Animals selected were picked for their intelligence, abilities and devotion to their masters. Within a few generations, litters of puppies would begin to look alike and the dogs would be able to perform specific tasks with a great deal of skill.

We know that the Belgian Tervuren is a Belgian dog and that his basic task was, and still is, to herd. With ease he can herd sheep or cattle and sometimes even his owner and family members, as the herding instinct lies deep within the breed. In addition to his herding abilities, the Belgian Tervuren excels in a number of other activities, such as agility, obedience, tracking, Schutzhund (protection training) and guarding.

Prior to the 1890s, the Belgian shepherds were not known as pure-bred dogs or as separate breeds or varieties but were known and used as working dogs on the farm. These dogs would herd and guard the livestock as well as protect their farmsteads and families.

In September 1891 the Club du Chien de Berger Belge (the Belgian Shepherd Dog Club) was formed in Belgium to decide if there was a shepherd dog that was representative of the country, such as the German Shepherd Dog is representative of Germany. On November 15, 1891, veterinarian Prof. Dr. Adolphe Reul assembled a group of individuals from the various Belgian counties to look over 117 representatives, and it was determined that there

Duc de Groenendael (drawing by Evan Gelder), the most famous son of Picard d'Uccle and Petite (the foundation couple of the Groenendael variety) and the father of Milsart, who played a major role in fixing the Tervuren type.

was a definite type of dog to represent Belgium. Forty dogs were selected from this group, all looking alike but with different coat lengths and coat colors.

Three of the Belgian shepherd varieties came to be named for the region of Belgium in which the variety originated. The Tervurens came from the town of

A nice typical Malinois at a Belgian dog show.

Tervuren, where they were originally bred by M. F. Corbeel. The Groenendaels were named after the chateau and kennel of Nicolas Rose, who bred the black Belgians. The Malinois were named after the city of Malines, where the majority of them were bred. The Laekenois, bred around Antwerp and Boom, were named after the kennel of their breeder, Adrien Janssen. The breeders of the Malinois valued the shorthaired variety of the Belgian sheepdog and focused primarily on the dogs' ability to work. Because Malinois were known for their working ability, the other types of Belgian shepherds were often interbred to Malinois.

In the United States there are three breeds of Belgians: the Malinois, the Tervuren and the Groenendael (called the Belgian Sheepdog in the US). All are called shepherd dogs and are shown in the American Kennel Club's (AKC) Herding Group. In Europe and the UK they are shown as four varieties (including the Laekenois) of one breed>. In the UK they are classified in the Pastoral Group; the Fédération Cynologique Internationale places them in Group 1 (Sheepdogs and Cattle Dogs except Swiss Cattle Dogs). In addition, the name "Tervuren" in the UK and Europe is spelled "Tervueren."

The Tervuren, the longhaired "other than black" Belgian shepherd, was for a long time treated as a poor cousin of the longhaired, solid-black Groenendael. It has been asserted incorrectly that the Tervuren was a cross-breeding of the Groenendael and the Collie. According to Louis Huyghebaert, Groenendaels and Tervurens have such a mutual relationship and a common origin that they cannot be separated. They are indeed the same dogs, only differing in color.

M. F. Corbeel, around 1895 in the town of Tervuren, owned two fawn-colored longhaired dogs named Tom and Poes. These two dogs are commonly considered the foundation breeding pair of the Tervuren variety. Tom and Poes produced Miss, a

fawn bitch with a good black overlay, and she was unquestionably regarded as the ancestor of the Belgian Tervuren.

Milsart, the result of the union of Miss and the black Duc de Groenendael, son of the black Groenendael foundation couple, Picard d'Uccle and Petite, played a major role in fixing the Tervuren type. In 1907 he became the first Tervuren champion. He had a deep charcoal fawn coat and has been described as a perfectly successful prototype of the variety; he is the real forefather of the charcoal fawn longhaired Belgian shepherd that became known as the Tervuren. His pedigree demonstrates the common origin of the two longhaired varieties, regardless of color, since all longhaired progeny definitely go back to Picard d'Uccle and Petite. Indeed, Tervurens born

The four varieties on a painting by A. Ackaert.

The Belgian Shepherds' cousin, the Schipperke, is known as "the little shepherd" and has been employed for various tasks, from herding to ratting.

**POST OFFICE SALUTES
BELGIUM'S TOP FOUR**
On May 26, 1986 four postage stamps
were issued in Belgium to honor the best-
known Belgian breeds, namely the Belgian
shepherd dogs (pictured, left to right:
Malinois, Tervuren and Groenendael) and
(not pictured) the Bouvier des Flandres.

haired, as seen in the Laekenois).
This Belgian standard was
reworked many times over the
years to reach its present format,
in which the four varieties of the
Belgian Shepherd Dog breed are
described, divided by coat
texture, coat color and length of
coat. In all other ways, the four
varieties are the same.

In 1898 a second club, the
Berger Belge Club, was formed in
Malines, Belgium. Due to
disputes, arguments and other
conflicts, discussions continued
about the coat types and colors,
in addition to controversy over
divergence in type between the
working dog and the dog bred for
the show ring. Eventually, Dr.
Reul's club disappeared and the
Berger Belge Club remained and
was recognized by the Société
Royale Saint-Hubert, the national
canine organization of Belgium.
Another club, the Royal
Groenendael Club, was also
recognized, and the two clubs
functioned until March of 1990
when they were finally united.

In the late 1890s, because the
Club du Chien de Berger Belge
held only herding trials, Louis
Huyghebaert began holding dres-
sage trials to test a Belgian's aptitude for jumping over high fences
and long obstacles and swimming
abilities. These trials were also
combined with protection work
and were called Belgian ring
sport (or campagnes). The first

from Groenendael parents have
played an essential part in the
development of the breed in
Europe.

From this short overview of
early history of the Belgian shepherds, it should be clear how
logical it is that the Belgian
Shepherd Dog is classified as one
single breed in Europe and the
UK. The four varieties, the result
of intermatings, are indeed only
different appearances of one and
the same dog.

On May 8, 1892 the first
Belgian specialty show was held
in Cureghem, Belgium. That
same year, the first standard for
the breed was written, describing
the three coat varieties (longhaired, as seen in the Tervuren
and Groenendael; shorthaired, as
seen in the Malinois; and rough-

trial was held in June of 1903 and ring trials became a fixture in Belgian shepherd society; national trials have been held on a yearly basis ever since.

Discussions over the colors of the various Belgian varieties began very early on. The three coat types had been established, but in 1901 the Société Royale Saint-Hubert accepted the long coat only in black, the short coat only in blackened fawn and the rough coat only in ash gray; the name designations (Groenendael, Malinois and Laekenois, respectively) for the varieties followed. However, some breeders would not accept this and bred outside these color rules. In 1914 a longhaired gray bitch was shown, and the exhibitors and breeders were totally taken with her. She was of exceptional beauty with a wonderful nature, and she embodied what the breeders were looking for in the breed. It was then decided that breeding should not be done for color alone but instead to produce the finest example of the breed. The long-haired fawn variety was not called "Tervuren" from the start, but eventually the name of the foundation breeder's hometown was the accepted name for the variety.

With the onset of World War I, discussions and disagreements between the various breeders subsided. With what little stock survived the war, breeding of Belgians began again, and the

red-brown and gray longhaired dogs were allowed into the breeding program. In 1920 the breed definitions changed and all colors that had been formerly eliminated were once again allowed and interbreeding between the varieties was again permitted.

In Belgium in 1921 two Belgian shepherds, Minox and Colette ex Folette, from four generations of Malinois, were bred and produced a litter of three Tervurens. These three dogs became the primary dogs in the

The four varieties of Belgian shepherd dogs.

MY COUSIN, THE SKIPPER
Let's not forget the "little Belgian shepherd," the Belgian cousin of the shepherd breeds, the Schipperke. It is generally accepted that the Belgian breed known as the Schipperke, a wholly black little shepherd dog (Schipperke means "little shepherd" in the Flemish dialect), and the Belgian shepherds have a common ancestor in the Leuvenaar. This extinct Belgian breed, whose name means "inhabitant of Louvain," was an all-black lupoid dog weighing between 22 and 26.5 pounds (10 and 12 kg). From this common stem, the smallest were selected as rat-catchers (Schipperkes) and the largest for herding and guarding livestock (Belgian shepherds).

development of both the Tervuren and the Groenendael. However, through interbreeding of the varieties, Tervurens kept showing up in Malinois litters, and this interbreeding was to continue for many years. Even at the present time there is a certain amount of controversy as to the interbreeding between the Malinois, Groenendael and Tervuren.

In 1922 the first Tervuren was registered in Switzerland, a bitch by the name of Dora, owned by Dr. Masson. Two more were registered in 1924 and 1925, also belonging to Dr. Masson. In 1935 Dr. Masson imported another Tervuren bitch from France to enhance his breeding program.

With the onset of World War II, as had happened during World War I, the breed took another decided drop in popularity. During World War II the Belgian shepherds were used in military service as well as by the Red Cross, whom they led to the wounded in the battlefields. Because the dogs were so skilled at their jobs, the German army was ordered to shoot the dogs on sight, which led to the near extinction of the breed. Thankfully a few breeders in Europe were able to hide their dogs and the Belgian shepherds did survive.

Few people realize that after the devastation of the breed

DIAGRAM OF MALINOIS AND LAEKENOIS ORIGINS

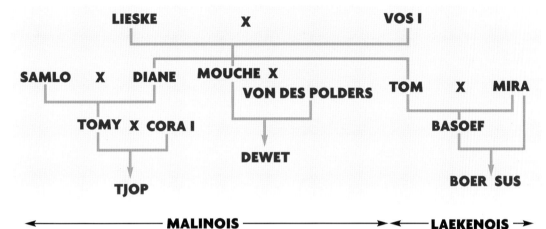

MALINOIS ← ———————————— → ← LAEKENOIS →

during World War II, America, almost as much as France, helped to recreate the Tervuren. Unfortunately, the European experts called the revived breed the "American type" of Tervuren, which is heavier, longer and more angulated than the European dog.

After World War II, the Tervuren started to become more popular. In 1946 the Swiss kennels of de la Tour Ronde and v. Hummelwald were breeding dogs, from imported Belgian animals, with outstanding temperaments and excellent conformation for the show ring. A standout dog was Urvinioul Deprez, who, with his excellent body, exceptional temperament and correct head and ears, was something that the breed was in need of at the time.

Whelped in 1948, Will de la Garde Noire was an outstanding example of the longhaired Belgian, and he was able to compete with the Malinois and the Groenendael on equal footing. Through the early 1950s "Willy" was instrumental in the development of the Tervuren as we know it today.

This Laekenois is multi-champion and World Champion Max van Kriekebos (Hassan van Kriekebos X Jody van Kriekebos).

THE BELGIAN TERVUREN COMES TO AMERICA

Although the Tervuren did not become popular in the US until after World War II, it came to America at a much earlier date, as the first Tervuren was registered with the American Kennel Club around 1920. The dog's name was Cesar, and he was registered by Oliver Ormsby Page. Page bred the dog to a Groenendael, and a litter of longhaired black and fawn puppies was produced. However, with the Great Depression and World War II, showing activity in the Tervuren was almost nonexistent, with the few that came into the country being registered as Belgian Sheepdogs, the breed name under which all of the varieties were registered in the US at that time. There had been a breed club, the Belgian Sheepdog Club of America (BSCA), which had encompassed the different varieties. This club dissolved in the early 1930s during the Great Depression, but a new BSCA was established in 1949.

By the 1940s several individuals were working together to get the Tervuren established as a breed in America. Rudy Robinson of Candide kennels in Wheaton, Illinois, who started breeding Groenendaels in 1947, corresponded with several well-known Belgian breeders in Europe.

An American-bred Belgian Groenendael.

During the following decades the Tervuren became more popular throughout the European countries. The breed established a following of fanciers and breeders who did much to improve the Belgian Tervuren and to establish it as a breed to be reckoned with not only in the show ring but also as a working dog, excelling in such activities as herding trials, Schutzhund and search and rescue. With their beauty, great versatility and skill as working dogs, it is obvious why the Belgian shepherds, in all colors and coat types, have remained beloved dogs in their native country of Belgium as well as throughout the world.

In 1953 he imported three Tervurens from the Saint Jacques kennel in France, and he continued to import Tervurens until his last pair came from France in 1959. Mr. Robinson is credited with the foundation of the Tervuren breed in the US and is recognized for his invaluable contributions to both the Tervuren and the Groenendael.

An American-bred Belgian Tervuren.

BSCA, as they were considered to be inferior. As other varieties were imported, more issues arose. At this point, the Tervuren was not even listed as a variety in the AKC standard for the Belgian Sheepdog. However, the Tervuren variety of the Belgian Sheepdog was becoming preferred by the public, as this variety started to win over the Malinois and Groenendaels in the ring. In June of 1958 D'Jimmy de Clos Saint-Clair, one

The Tervuren is a longhaired Belgian shepherd that is "rich fawn to russet mahogany with black overlay."

The 1950s brought about controversy and change. During the years between 1953 and 1959, the BSCA's newsletter wrote very little about the history and genetics of the Belgian varieties or the interbreeding between them, and nothing had been written about their common ancestors. In addition, the foreign Groenendaels were not welcomed by the

As a puppy, the Belgian Tervuren possesses a softer coat than the adult.

DIAGRAM OF GROENENDAEL AND TERVUREN ORIGINS

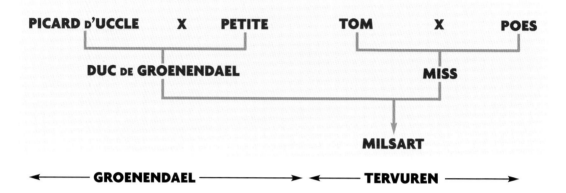

PICARD D'UCCLE   X   **PETITE**   **TOM**   X   **POES**

DUC DE GROENENDAEL   **MISS**

MILSART

←———— **GROENENDAEL** ————→ ←—— **TERVUREN** ——→

of Rudy Robinson's imports, became the first Tervuren to gain his championship in America.

A group of Groenendael breeders protested to the American Kennel Club that the varieties were not the same breed and should not all be registered together as Belgian Sheepdogs. At the request of the Groenendael breeders, the AKC polled the Belgian Sheepdog owners about inter-variety breeding and conformation competition. In July 1959, with a poor response to the questionnaire, the AKC board voted that only the Groenendael variety would retain the breed name Belgian Sheepdog. This marked the official separation of the three varieties. The Tervuren and Malinois were now called by the breed names "Belgian Tervuren" and "Belgian Malinois," and the

American Kennel Club allowed separate breed clubs to be formed. Also in July 1959, separate breed standards for the Belgian Sheepdog, Belgian Tervuren and Belgian Malinois were approved by the AKC. At this time the Malinois was relegated to the Miscellaneous Class; its numbers became sufficient for readmittance into the Working Group in 1965. The Lakenois, with insignificant numbers in the US, was not considered for AKC acceptance.

Although the breed standards have been reworked over the years, to this day the three breeds are still anatomically the same, with some differences in size and certainly differences in coat. At this time, however, there is still considerable debate in the US regarding interbreeding among the breeds.

Ch. Scorpio de Fauve Charbonne CD, TD, owned by Joyce Henry, bred by Bob and Barbara Krohn. Scorpio was the 1972 American Belgian Tervuren Club's national specialty BOB winner.

Bob and Barbara Krohn of Fauve Charbonne kennels were the force behind the new American Belgian Tervuren Club (ABTC), which began with just 12 charter members. The Krohns, along with Rudy Robinson, were very important contributors to the Tervuren in the early days and onward. The Krohns owned one of Mr. Robinson's imported Groenendaels when he began importing Tervurens, and he had arranged for them to take one of his first imported Tervs, the bitch Chrysis du Clos Saint Jacques. Chrysis was the first Tervuren to earn the Companion Dog (CD) title in obedience, and she produced offspring that became foundation stock for other important American kennels.

The Krohns are also credited with the most influential Tervuren litter ever produced, the "K" litter by Dandy du Clos Saint Jacques out of the imported Jasmine de Cledeville. The two dogs and three bitches in this litter all became champions, and the three females became the foundation bitches for the Georjune, Chateau Blanc and Bonheur kennels.

Katie de Fauve Charbonne went to the Georjune kennels of June Betsworth, who had been previously breeding German

Am./Can. Ch. Hi Times Kanook of Crocs Blanc CD, shown winning Best in Show at Colorado Springs KC in 1975 under judge Joe Gregory, owner-handled by Judith Lee Smith. Kanook won six Bests in Show in the US between 1972-1976 and another BIS in Canada. He was also a specialty BIS winner.

Shepherd Dogs. She was the first "K" bitch to be bred. Out of Katie's first litter came 1971's top-producing sire, Ch. Joker of Georjune, who was also the first North American Group-winning Tervuren with a Group One in Canada. June's breeding and showing lasted through the 1970s, but her impact on the Tervuren is still felt today. The quality of her breeding program, which produced many multi-titled champions and obedience winners, lives on in the kennels that started on Georjune foundation stock.

Chateau Blanc kennels of the Laurin family in Connecticut started in the early 1960s with the foundation pair Ch. Flair de Fauve Charbonne CD, BAR and Ch. Kandice de Fauve Charbonne CDX, BAR from the "K" litter. They were bred together three times, and offspring from these pairings became cornerstones of not just their bloodline but of the Tervuren as a whole. Kandice was the first Belgian Tervuren bitch to earn a championship and a CDX title in obedience. Since its beginnings, Chateau

.begin

Blanc has always emphasized the all-around Tervuren, titling dogs in conformation and a multitude of performance events. Over 20 of their dogs have earned the BAR award, and their dogs are always breeder/owner-handled.

Note that the BAR designation after a dog's or bitch's name denotes Breeder Achievement Record, an award indicating an outstanding producer of both breed and obedience progeny as determined by the American Belgian Tervuren Club.

Kriquette de Fauve Charbonne, the third of the "K" litter bitches, went to the Dickens family in Virginia in 1962 to start their Bonheur kennels. Kriquette was successfully shown and was part of the first all-champion Tervuren litter. Her first litter produced several champions as well as the first Tervuren to achieve a perfect score in obedience. This kennel later bred the first Tervuren to win an all-breed Best in Show, Ch. Bonheur's D'Artagnan UDT, BAR. Another milestone for the kennel was when Ch. Bonheur Star Treader CDX, TD became the first dog of any breed to go Best in Show from the AKC's Herding Group (following the AKC's division of the Working Group into two groups, Working and Herding).

Sallyann Comstock of Sanroyale kennels in Texas

.

DUTCH COUSINS
The Belgian Shepherds have many admirers in the Netherlands despite that country's indigenous herding dog, the Dutch Shepherd. This handsome herder occurs in three coat types, long, rough and short, just like its neighbor, the Belgian. The breed is more colorful, including blue, gray, yellow, silver and various eye-catching shades of brindle. Of the three varieties, the short coat is the most popular, though all three are unfortunately very rare, even in Holland.

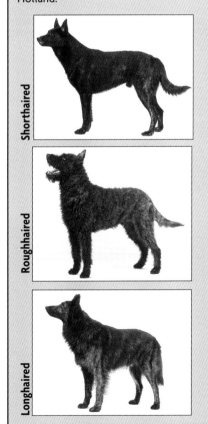

Shorthaired

Roughhaired

Longhaired

The top-winning Ch. Corsairs Beaujangles C/O-BAR shown winning one of his record 24 all-breed Bests in Show under judge Maxine Beam at Monroe Kennel Club in 1983, owner-handled by Steve Sorensen.

Ch. Quincey du Garde Roux, shown winning Best in Show under judge Winifred Heckman in the early 1970s.

started in Great Danes and Dobermans but in 1965 saw her first Tervuren and began looking into the breed's characteristics.

By 1966 she purchased her foundation bitch from Dorothy Hollister of Val de Tonnere Belgians. Ms. Comstock has bred many fine dogs but special mention should be made of the following: Best in Show Am./Can. Ch. Rajah D'Antre du Louve CD, BAR; Int. Ch. Our Valiant du Sanroyale; and Am./Bermuda Ch. Sanroyale's the Hustler CD, BAR.

Cachet Noir (formerly called Starburst kennels), the New Hampshire kennel of Dana MacKoni, bred Ch. StarBright Bonne Chance CDX, Am./Can.

TD, HIC, PD1, PD2, BAR-CX, whelped in 1978. He produced Best in Show and specialty Best in Show winners as well as working dogs who achieved obedience High in Trials and herding-trial wins.

Larry and Sue Mills of Ques-Que-Ce kennels in Elmira, Oregon got their first Tervuren in 1971 and since that time have bred and handled many conformation champions in addition to putting a number of Working Certificates on their dogs. Among their best was Am./Can. Ch. Ques-Que-Ce's Keeper Of The Flame, a big winner and a marvelously balanced, sound and typey Tervuren. In addition, the Millses are active in the rescue and rehoming of Belgian Tervurens.

Steve Sorenson from Eau Claire, Wisconsin bred and owned the dog that has been the top-winning Belgian Tervuren to date. Steve bred, conditioned and showed Ch. Corsairs Beaujangles C/O-BAR, whelped in 1979, to 24 all-breed Bests in Show and 95 Group Ones. Beau was the national specialty Best of Breed in 1983, number-one Belgian all-systems in 1982, 1983, 1984 and 1985 and the first winner of the newly formed Herding Group at Westminster in 1983. Beau was a confident and impressive dog and was always shown in peak condition. In addition to Beaujangles, Steve

Best of Breed at Westminster in 2000 under breeder judge Edeltraud Laurin was Ch. Sunset's Orion After Dark, handled by Teresa Nash. Owned by Diane Dykman.

Ch. Bonheur Star Treader, a multiple-BIS winner in the 1980s, shown winning at Vacationland Dog Club in 1986 under judge Dr. Samuel Draper. Star Treader was owned by N. and J. Rose and handled by Roger Ellis.

Eng. Ch. Vallivue Bon Chance was a top-winning Tervuren in the UK with a Crufts Group win to his credit.

has also showed the home-bred Ch. Corsairs Wizard and Ch. Corsairs Paragon to all-breed Bests in Show.

Since the new millennium the Belgian Tervuren has continued its winning ways in many endeavors, including conformation, herding, tracking, agility, obedience and Rally.

The national club did an extensive health survey in 2003 in which 279 owners responded with health information on 633 Tervurens, updating the previous health survey which took place in 1998. In addition the club revised the Belgian Tervuren breed stan-

dard in 2007. The results of the health survey and the standard can be found on the Internet at www.abtc.org. The national club also maintains an active rescue committee to make certain that every Tervuren finds a good and suitable home.

In the conformation field, the top winner for the past three years has been Ch. Magic's Ty Won On At Char-Ma, bred by Gail Gombos-Smith and owned by Frank and Charlene Masuch. He was the top-wining dog for 2003, 2004 and 2005, winning 11 all-breed Bests in Show. Ch. Sky Acres Piper Aerostar, bred and owned by Michelle Edling, was also an all-breed Best in Show dog.

Since 2004, four Tervs have achieved their conformation championships in addition to adding the coveted tracking degree to their names. They are Ch. CT Summerstorm Heart Desire AX, AXJ, Ch. CT O-Tahn-Agon Cinema Duet, Ch. CT Symon's Treasure Issi VCD2, UD, PT, CGC and Ch. CT Corsair's Vogue De Serimar OA, OAJ. Serimar comes from Steve Sorenson's kennel, home of Ch. Corsairs Beaujangles C/O-BAR, the top-winning Terv of all time.

Another dog to receive the highest honor in the breed is Ch. OTCh. MACH Chateau d'Vie's Hors de Pair, owned and trained by Julie Symons, bred by Andrea Meinhart and Jody Bradley. He is the first Tervuren to earn his conformation championship, his Obedience Trial Championship (OTCh.) and his Master Agility Championship (MACH). The Belgian Tervuren continues his work as a most capable dog of excelling in many areas of activity.

Of course, there are many more who have been and continue to be important to the Tervuren breed in the US. The Belgian Tervuren has been fortunate in having dedicated foundation breeders as well as current responsible breeders who continually work toward raising healthy, intelligent and sturdy stock. They not only work their dogs in the variety of fields in

World Ch. Sherpa van de Hoge Laer was a striking and popular international winner.

TOPS IN EUROPE

In Belgium, Ch. Quowboy du Long Spinoy, whelped in 1967, was the winner of 57 CACIB and 26 CAC certificates and was selected in 1969 as a recommended stud dog. RE Belg./Fr./Nl./Lux./Int. Ch. Grimm van de Hoge Laer, whelped in 1982, was a winner both in the ring and with his working abilities as well as being an outstanding producer of winning and working dogs. He was considered one of the outstanding Tervurens. RE Fr./Euro./Lux. Ch. Ares du Bois du Tot, whelped in France in 1985, won the French championship four times and was the Best Producer in France in 1991 and 1993.

which Belgians can excel but they also show their dogs throughout the country so that the public can see what a beautiful and exceptional breed the Tervuren is. The motto of the American Belgian Sheepdog Club, which notes that the breed is rare but well established, is, "A well-balanced Tervuren has a Ch. (championship) on one end and a UDT (Utility Dog Tracker) on the other."

THE BELGIAN SHEPHERD DOG IN BRITAIN

In 1965 the Belgian Shepherd Dog Association was formed in the UK. At that time, only the

Groenendael variety was in the country, because it had been decided to import only the black longhaired Groenendael, not the red longhaired Tervuren, to avoid confusion with the longhaired German Shepherd Dog. In 1972 the first Groenendael arrived from the United States, and from 1975 on, new and regular imports came from Belgium and France. By the 1980s, even the rarer Laekenois was established in the UK.

In 1971 the first Tervuren imports to England came from France and also from the US. In fact, the early development of the Tervuren in Britain was dominated by American imports, which differed in type from the Continental dogs. The American dogs lacked overall elegance and had less-refined heads. Fortunately, imports from Belgium during the years from 1978 to 1983 had a great impact and the quality of British Belgian Shepherds was markedly improved.

The popularity of all four varieties was growing steadily. However, England's The Kennel Club had been unhappy with matings between the varieties and in 1994 decided that all Belgian Shepherd Dogs would be shown in the ring as one breed, not as one breed with four distinct varieties. This proved to be a mistake. The breeders of each variety lost heart, and breeding reached a

| **A WELL-KEPT SECRET** |
| Although the Tervuren's qualities are great, its popularity remains higher in Europe than in America, with AKC registrations placing it around 100th in popularity among AKC-recognized breeds. A full list of AKC registered breeds and their rankings can be found in the "Registrations" section of the American Kennel Club's website: www.akc.org. For more about the Tervuren, visit the American Belgian Tervuren Club online at www.abtc.org. |

virtual standstill. The only variety not to sustain serious damage was the Tervuren.

By 1999 The Kennel Club realized what was happening and approached the Northern Belgian Shepherd Dog Club and the Belgian Shepherd Dog Association, asking them to poll their members. The results were in favor of reverting to the previous status of four varieties, shown separately, with no inter-variety matings. The Kennel Club accepted this, and the first show of this kind was held at Crufts in 2000.

The Tervuren had been making an impact in Britain since the late 1980s. Belamba Tervurens bred the first British Tervuren champion, Eng. Ch. Belamba Bianco at Vallivue, as well as Britain's first gray champion, Eng.

Ch. Norrevang Bacchus of Belamba. Bacchus sired Eng. Ch. Vallivue Bon Chance, winner of 42 Challenge Certificates and a Group at Crufts. He is in the background of over 35 British champions, and through his semen's being imported to Australia he has champion offspring in that country as well. Eng. Ch. France de la Douce Plaine of Belamba was whelped in 1990 and came to Belamba kennels from France; she won 12 Challenge Certificates and was the 8th top brood bitch all-breeds in the UK. Her offspring were sent to America and to Australia, where there are champion progeny on both continents. These are just some of the Tervuren milestones achieved by Belamba kennels.

Eng. Ch. Opium Van de Hoge Laer at Corsini was imported to Britain's Corsini kennels in 1990 from the famous Van de Hoge Laer kennels in Belgium. In addition to his own achievements in the show ring, "Carlos" was the top Belgian Shepherd stud dog (all varieties) in Britain for five

years beginning in 1996; that year, he was also the ninth top stud dog all-breeds. He was the sire of many well-known British Tervuren champions. Twenty Tervuren champions have been bred under Amanda McLaren's Corsini prefix; Ms. McLaren has also been active in the Belgian Shepherd Dog Association of Great Britain and has judged the breed around the world at shows including breed specialties and prestigious international events.

Another significant Tervuren in the variety's British history was Eng. Ch. Bergerac Sweet Talk Dash. Whelped in 1988, she won seven Challenge Certificates and was the dam of the top-winning Tervuren in 1998 and 1999.

Whatever the color or coat variety, all Belgian shepherd dogs have the same basic characteristics.

CHARACTERISTICS OF THE
BELGIAN TERVUREN

Tervurens and children can form strong bonds as long as they know how to treat each other with care and respect. All child-dog interactions must be supervised by an adult.

The Belgian Tervuren is a fairly large-sized dog but smaller than a German Shepherd Dog and more refined. He is an extremely smart dog and a quick learner who will demand an owner who is as smart and as quick as he is. He will be a wonderful companion for the owner who is looking for an active and versatile dog. The Tervuren has the potential to excel in such dog sports as agility, obedience, herding trials and even therapy work. If this is the kind of family member you are looking for, the Tervuren may be the dog for you.

Do be aware, however, that the Tervuren is not the dog for everyone. As a puppy, he will be easy to pick up and cuddle, and he will be as cute a puppy as you will want. However, in addition to attention and affection, the young Terv will need to be socialized, and you also must be aware of the breed's sensitivities. Tervurens form such strong attachment to their owners that they can even become a little "needy," especially in puppyhood. Further, they are very sensitive to their owners' tone of voice and do not do well with harsh reprimands. The positive side of this is he responds well to praise and approval and will be eager to please you. The Tervuren's devotion to his master is legendary.

Although not typically a "hyper" dog, the Tervuren has a high energy level and loves doing things with his owner. He needs an owner who understands this and has the time and

The Tervuren needs a generous amount of exercise for both his mind and his body. A good way to ensure plenty of exercise is to add another Tervuren to the mix.

acceptance to work with this type of canine. The Tervuren needs ample exercise every day, including daily on-leash walks and, if possible, free-running and play in a safely enclosed area. This is not a breed that you can let lie around the house. If underexercised, bored or not given enough attention, a Tervuren will find his own activities and ways to entertain himself, which will probably not be to your liking. This can be the cause of destructive and/or compulsive behaviors like chewing, scratching, tail chasing, barking, etc.

All reputable Tervuren breeders count temperament as one of the most important traits they breed for. Breeders want to produce dogs who not only can do a job but who also have even temperaments and get along well in their human families. A Terv must never be nervous, aggressive, fearful or snappish. However, because this is considered a "protection" breed, he will defend his home and his family when necessary. And again, do be aware that since Tervurens are possessive of and devoted to their families, they can be demanding of their people's attention.

The Belgian's behavior sets him apart from other shepherd breeds. His rapid reflexes, impulsiveness, emotionality and hypersensitivity are very distinctive. His "qualities of character," which are vital for his success as a working dog, find expression in his general appearance and have been described as follows in the author's *The Blueprint of the Belgian Shepherd Dog*: "The sparkling temperament…should be shown in his whole attitude and expression. He is always ready for action. His athletic body looks full of explosive forces which he finds difficult to contain. They persuade us of their strength, their intrepidity and their readiness to pass into action. All this attitude of body and the specific expression of the head and eyes are very typical of the breed."

Children in the household must be introduced to the new puppy carefully, and it is very important that they understand, before the dog is brought home, that they must treat the dog in a respectful manner. Children must be taught that they cannot scare the pup, grab at the puppy or roughhouse with the puppy. It is very important that there be an adult supervising play periods between the children and the dog to ensure that they behave properly with each other. You must be aware of this before purchasing your Tervuren puppy. However, it is easier to introduce a young puppy, rather than an adult dog, into the family.

The American Belgian Malinois Club states the following, which also can be said about the Tervuren: "The Belgian Malinois is at his best when given a job, but it is equally important to integrate the Malinois into family life by setting clear behavior guidelines as well as training him to behave as a 'Canine Good Citizen' whether at home, with guests or strangers or in the park." Just replace "Malinois" with "Tervuren"—the same guidelines apply. Remember, this is a smart breed. If you don't set the rules for the puppy when he is very young, you will have a Tervuren

A MODEL COMPANION

The Belgian Tervuren has many outstanding qualities to offer the right owners:
- Intelligence, versatility and attractiveness, he has the potential for success in many pursuits: conformation showing, performance events (obedience, agility, herding, tracking and more), therapy-dog work, etc.
- For those not interested in specialized training, this is still an active dog who can and loves to do much with his owners
- Natural beauty and elegance that appeals to many
- Overall sound health and longevity: average lifespan of 12 to 14 years is long for the breed's size
- Willingness to please and ability to learn
- Affectionate nature and loyalty toward owners
- Alert and watchful; protective of his family, home and property.

running your household! But if you understand the breed and enjoy teaching and doing things with your dog, the Tervuren is one of the most rewarding dogs you can own.

PHYSICAL CHARACTERISTICS

To be able to do their job properly, shepherd dogs should be of medium build. The Belgian shepherds and other similar breeds have features that can be described as "lupine" or "wolf-like," such as their erect ears, pointed muzzles and bushy tails. While the Belgian shepherds were originally bred for herding ability

only, the increasing popularity of dog shows made breeders and the public pay more attention to appearance. The Belgian shepherds are beautiful dogs, with four different coat and color combinations. While the Belgian Malinois is likely the best known of the breeds, the red or fawn Tervuren with black overlay is considered by many to be the most beautiful.

When comparing the physical appearance of the Belgian Tervuren (or that of the other Belgian shepherds, as the only variation is in coat and color) with other shepherd dogs, it is obvious that very important

A natural herding and protection dog, the Tervuren still excels in his pastoral duties.

anatomical characteristics, such as the Tervuren's rather light skeleton, moderate angulation and overall elegant appearance, are most favorable for a working dog. The Tervuren is also very quick and agile, with impressive jumping and climbing ability.

BREED-SPECIFIC HEALTH CONCERNS

There are hereditary health problems in most breeds of dog, and the Tervuren is no exception. While most Tervurens will not be affected by hereditary problems, as a potential Tervuren owner you must be aware of the problems that exist in the breed. Be sure to buy your puppy from a reputable breeder and discuss these health issues with your breeder. The breeder should be willing to discuss honestly the occurrence of any hereditary problems in his bloodline and should be able to show you documentation of appropriate health testing on his breeding animals.

HIP AND ELBOW DYSPLASIA

Hip dysplasia exists in the Tervuren, as it does in most, especially larger, breeds. Hip dysplasia is an inherited disease in which the head of the femur (thigh bone) fails to fit into the socket of the hip bone and there is not enough muscle mass to hold the joint together. All Tervurens that are bred should have healthy hips as

determined by an x-ray evaluation done by the Orthopedic Foundation for Animals (OFA). Dogs with good hips are issued an OFA number; ask the breeder to see this certification on the parents of the puppy you are considering.

Depending on the severity, the symptoms can differ. Some dogs may adapt well to the condition and not show obvious changes while other dogs will be in more pain and will move with great difficulty, perhaps even becoming crippled. Because sometimes the symptoms are not obvious, it is important for all Tervurens to have their hips x-rayed.

Thankfully the occurrence of hip dysplasia in the Terv is low when compared to other breeds. However, even if the problem is less prevalent than in other breeds, it does not mean that breeders can be careless with their breeding programs. They must continue to breed healthy, OFA-certified animals to one another.

Elbow dysplasia, which is also a hereditary disease, can occur in the Tervuren as well. In fact, it is thought that the incidence of elbow dysplasia in the breed is higher than that of hip dysplasia. Again, x-rays should be taken of the animals that are to be bred and sent to the OFA for evaluation. The OFA issues certification numbers for healthy elbows as it does for hips. Ask to see

Do You Know about Hip Dysplasia?

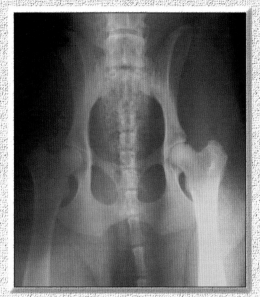

X-ray of a dog with "Good" hips.

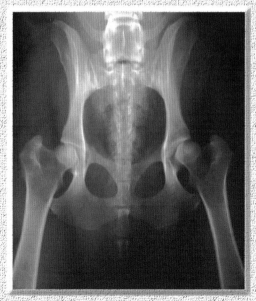

X-ray of a dog with "Moderate" dysplastic hips.

Hip dysplasia is a fairly common condition found in pure-bred dogs. When a dog has hip dysplasia, his hind leg has an incorrectly formed hip joint. By constant use of the hip joint, it becomes more and more loose, wears abnormally and may become arthritic.

Hip dysplasia can only be confirmed with an x-ray, but certain symptoms may indicate a problem. Your dog may have a hip dysplasia problem if he walks in a peculiar manner, hops instead of smoothly runs, uses his hind legs in unison (to keep the pressure off the weak joint), has trouble getting up from a prone position or always sits with both legs together on one side of his body.

As the dog matures, he may adapt well to life with a bad hip, but in a few years the arthritis develops and many dogs with hip dysplasia become crippled.

Hip dysplasia is considered an inherited disease and only can be diagnosed definitively by x-ray when the dog is two years old, although symptoms often appear earlier. Some experts claim that a special diet might help your puppy outgrow the bad hip, but the usual treatments are surgical. The removal of the pectineus muscle, the removal of the round part of the femur, reconstructing the pelvis and replacing the hip with an artificial one are all surgical interventions that are expensive, but they are usually very successful. Follow the advice of your veterinarian.

documentation that the sire and dam of your pup have healthy elbows as determined by the OFA.

PROGRESSIVE RETINAL ATROPHY
Progressive retinal atrophy (PRA) is an inherited condition that leads to the slow deterioration of the light-sensing ability of the retina, eventually resulting in total blindness of the dog. It is not thought to be an extensive problem in the breed; nonetheless, the American Belgian Tervuren Club advocates yearly eye exams and registration with CERF (the Canine Eye Registration Foundation). CERF keeps records of eye testing and the occurrence of eye disease in pure-bred dogs. Both parents of your pup should have had a CERF-certified eye exam within the past year. It is important for breeders to keep up with yearly eye exams. Testing of this frequency

is important since certain eye problems can present themselves at any time in a dog's life.

CANINE EPILEPSY
Idiopathic (of unknown cause) epilepsy is also seen in the Tervuren; in fact, it can occur in many dogs, pure-bred and mixed breed alike. In the Tervuren, the age of onset is typically between two and five years of age, with seizures occurring every few months. Seizures are the result of abnormal bursts of electrical activity within the brain; episodes usually last a few minutes, although the severity varies from dog to dog. This condition is a concern to all Tervuren breeders, since some dogs seem to have an inherited predisposition to epilepsy, yet the mode of inheritance is not known. The American Belgian Tervuren Club is participating in an extensive veterinary research study to help determine a genetic marker for the condition in hopes of eventually eradicating the disease.

Seizures are usually not life-threatening although they can be frightening to the onlooker. After your dog's first experience with a seizure, he should be taken to your veterinarian for an examination and a possible determination of the cause of the seizure, as well as to determine a treatment plan. Dogs who display seizure activity should not be bred.

BREED HEALTH AND THE ABTC
The American Belgian Tervuren Club (ABTC) has a very active health education committee that not only discusses the health issues of the breed but also keeps its members informed of any changes in information regarding inheritance factors and testing programs. The ABTC keeps its website, www.abtc.org, up to date with the latest health information, as do the clubs for the other Belgian shepherd breeds.

BREED STANDARD FOR THE
BELGIAN TERVUREN

When dogs were being shown for the first time at shows in the late 1800s, breeders realized that there must be more consistency within the breeds; the dogs in the ring should look alike as well as being of the same type as their sire and dam. This required an official description of the breed for breeders to use as a blueprint and for judges to use in the show ring. Standards were originally written by fanciers who had a profound knowledge of, love of and concern for the breed. They knew that the essential characteristics of the Belgian Tervuren must be maintained through the generations. As time progressed and breeders became more aware that certain areas of the dog needed a better description or more definition, breeders would meet together and work out a new standard. However, standards for any breed are not changed on a whim, and serious study and exchange between breeders take place before any move is made.

The American Kennel Club requires that each recognized breed have an official standard. A breed's standard gives the

reader a mental picture of what that breed should look and act like. All reputable breeders strive to produce animals that will meet the requirements of the standard. Many breeds were developed for a specific purpose, such as hunting, retrieving, going to ground, coursing, guarding, herding, etc.

The Tervuren's head should be long and well chiseled, boasting an intelligent, alert, inquisitive and ready expression.

Despite their rather different appearances, the Belgian shepherds are structurally identical except for coat and color.

The Belgian Tervuren, like all of the Belgian shepherd breeds, was originally bred for herding livestock and for protection of the flock, farm and family. In addition to having dogs that look like proper Belgian Tervurens, the standard assures that the breed will have the personality, disposition, skills and intelligence that have been sought after since the breed's beginnings.

The breed standard is useful for pet owners too. Even if he has no interest in showing his dog, a devotee of the breed will surely be curious as to how his dog measures up. The standard is also an educational tool with which the prospective owner should acquaint himself before beginning his search for a Tervuren. Whether his animal is a show, competition, working or pet dog, every Tervuren owner wants a dog that embodies the typical qualities of the breed.

In the United States, the Belgian Tervuren, Belgian Malinois and Belgian Sheepdog (Groenendael) are recognized as three separate breeds with three separate standards. In the UK and Fédération Cynologique Internationale countries, there is just one standard that covers the four varieties (including the Laekenois). Regardless, the only differences that exist between the breeds/varieties are coat and color; everything else is identical. Further, the standards of the different countries are very similar, which is important for preserving the breeds in a unified type around the world.

THE SAME BUT DIFFERENT
According to all of the standards, the desired characteristics of the Belgian breeds, without comment on coat length, texture or color, could read as follows: "An elegant square body; head long, wedge shaped, finely chiseled and carried highly; dark, almond-shaped eyes, lively look; small, triangular, stiff, upstanding ears; horizontal backline; croup only very slightly inclined; chest well let down, but upwards-curving underline (abdomen); sufficient angulation; movement firm and supple, with moderate stride; a sparkling temperament and a character assured, without fear whatsoever or aggressiveness."

AKC STANDARD FOR THE BELGIAN TERVUREN

General Appearance: The first impression of the Belgian Tervuren is that of a well balanced medium size dog, elegant in appearance, standing squarely on all fours, with proud carriage of head and neck. He is strong, agile, well muscled, alert and full of life. He gives the impression of depth and solidity without bulkiness. The male should appear unquestionably

The breed standard describes the ideal Tervuren, a dog that is sound and balanced in mind and body, with all of the traits necessary to do the work he was intended to do, whether or not he is used in a working capacity.

masculine; the female should have a distinctly feminine look and be judged equally with the male. The Belgian Tervuren is a natural dog and there is no need for excessive posing in the show ring.

The Belgian Tervuren reflects the qualities of intelligence, courage, alertness and devotion to master. In addition to his inherent ability as a herding dog, he protects his master's person and property without being overtly aggressive. He is watchful, attentive, and usually in motion when not under command.

The Belgian Tervuren is a herding dog, and faults which affect his ability to herd under all conditions, such as poor gait, bite, coat or temperament should be particularly penalized.

Size, Proportion, Substance: The ideal male is 24 to 26 inches in height and female 22 to 24 inches in height measured at the withers. Dogs are to be penalized in accordance to the degree they deviate from the ideal. Males under 23 inches or over 26.5 inches or females under 21 inches or over 24.5 inches are to be disqualified. The body is square; the length measured from the point of shoulder to the point of the rump approximates the height. Females may be somewhat longer in body. Bone structure is medium in proportion to height, so that he is well balanced

NOT ANOTHER GERMAN SHEPHERD DOG

Many are inclined to think that the Belgian Tervuren, indeed all of the Belgian shepherd breeds, and the German Shepherd Dog are very similar. However, when comparing the Belgian breeds to the German Shepherd, the distinguishing features of the Belgian breeds are:

• A lighter skeleton, more elegant appearance and high carriage of the head
• The impression of refinement of the finely chiseled head, which means that the head should not be coarse or heavy but dry with close-fitting, not slack or wrinkled, skin and with clean-cut lines and contours
• The square outline; he is not longer than tall; the body, from the front of the chest to the back of the buttocks, fits into a square, not into an oblong
• The angulation (the angles formed at the joints by the meeting of the bones) is moderate to normal, not excessive as in many German Shepherds; consequently, the Belgian's hind legs are well under the body when the dog is standing or in show stance
• The rather short length of reach or the short strides referring to the distance covered with each stride when trotting; this is a consequence of the square body structure and the moderate angulation of the fore- and the hindquarters.

A mature specimen in full coat showing proper balance, type and substance—with a typically alert and intelligent demeanor.

throughout and neither spindly or leggy nor cumbersome and bulky.

Head: Well chiseled, skin taut, long without exaggeration. *Expression*—intelligent and questioning, indicating alertness, attention and readiness for action. *Eyes*—dark brown, medium size, slightly almond shape, not protruding. Light, yellow or round eyes are a fault. *Ears*—triangular in shape, well cupped, stiff, erect, height equal to width at base. Set high, the base of the ear does not come below the center of the eye. Hanging ears, as on a hound, are a disqualification. *Skull and muzzle*—measuring from the stop are of equal length. Overall size is in proportion to the body, top of skull flattened rather than rounded, the width approximately the same as, but not wider than the length. *Stop*—moderate. The topline of the muzzle is parallel to the topline of the skull when viewed from the side. Muzzle moderately pointed, avoiding any tendency toward snipiness or cheekiness. *Jaws* strong and powerful. *Nose* black without spots or discolored areas. Nostrils well defined. *Lips* tight and black, no pink showing on the outside when mouth is closed. *Teeth*—Full complement of strong white teeth,

Head study of a mature dog showing correct structure, proportion, type and proper alert and intelligent intensity.

with no loose folds. Withers accentuated. *Topline* level, straight and firm from withers to croup. Croup medium long, sloping gradually to the base of the tail. Chest not broad without being narrow, but deep; the lowest point of the brisket reaching the elbow, forming a smooth ascendant curve to the abdomen. *Abdomen* moderately developed, neither tucked up nor paunchy. Ribs well sprung but flat on the sides. Loin section viewed from above is relatively short, broad and strong, but blending smoothly into the back. *Tail* strong at the base, the last vertebra to reach at least to the hock. At rest the dog holds it low, the tip bent back level with the hock. When in action, he may raise it to a point level with the topline giving it a slight curve, but not a hook. Tail is not carried above the backline nor turned to one side. A cropped or stump tail is a disqualification.

evenly set, meeting in a scissors or a level bite. Overshot and undershot teeth are a fault. Undershot teeth such that contact with the upper incisors is lost by two or more of the lower incisors is a disqualification. Loss of contact caused by short center incisors in an otherwise correct bite shall not be judged undershot. Broken or discolored teeth should not be penalized. Missing teeth are a fault.

Neck, Topline, Body: *Neck* round, muscular, rather long and elegant, slightly arched and tapered from head to body. Skin well fitting

Forequarters: *Shoulders* long, laid back 45 degrees, flat against the body, forming a right angle with the upper arm. Top of the shoulder blades roughly two thumbs width apart. Upper arms should move in a direction exactly parallel to the longitudinal axis of the body. *Forearms* long and well muscled. Legs straight and parallel, perpendicular to the ground. Bone oval rather than round. Pasterns short and strong, slightly

---

sloped. Dewclaws may be removed. *Feet* rounded, cat footed, turning neither in nor out, toes curved close together, well padded, strong nails.

Hindquarters: *Legs* powerful without heaviness, moving in the same pattern as the limbs of the forequarters. Bone oval rather than round. Thighs broad and heavily muscled. *Stifles* clearly defined, with upper shank at right angles to hip bones. *Hocks* moderately bent. Metatarsi short, perpendicular to the ground, parallel to each other when viewed from the rear. Dewclaws are removed. *Feet* slightly elongated, toes curved close together, heavily padded, strong nails.

Coat: The Belgian Tervuren is particularly adaptable to extremes of temperature or climate. The guard hairs of the coat must be long, close fitting, straight and abundant. The texture is of medium harshness, not silky or wiry. Wavy or curly hair is undesirable. The undercoat is very dense, commensurate, however, with climatic conditions. The hair is short on the head, outside the ears, and on the front part of the legs. The opening of the ear is protected by tufts of hair. *Ornamentation* consists of especially long and abundant hair, like a collarette around the neck, particularly on males; fringe of long hair down the back of the forearm; especially long and abundant hair trimming the breeches; long, heavy and abundant hair on the tail. *The female rarely has as long or as ornamented a coat as the male. This disparity must not be a consideration when the female is judged against the male.*

WARNING, WARNING

We have to warn about a possible divergence of the type of the four varieties into four different appearances. In *The Blueprint of the Belgian Shepherd Dog*, written by the author, it states: "Although the coats and color differentiate the varieties, it is well known that the danger exists that the four varieties would develop into different types. It would be a very bad thing for the Belgian Shepherd if the four varieties had already developed so much that there would be in reality four types, and that going back to the original type would not be possible anymore."

In Belgium and in many other countries, it is possible, in order to ensure that the type does not diverge, to obtain permission for inter-variety breeding when the request from the breeder is supported by serious and strong arguments. Therefore, in FCI countries and the UK, a longhaired fawn (Tervuren) puppy, bred from Groenendael parents, should be registered as a Tervuren and not as a "red Groenendael."

FAULTS IN PROFILE

Generally lacking in bone, substance and soundness—snipey muzzle, ewe-necked, upright shoulders, narrow front, shallow-chested, soft topline, narrow and cow-hocked behind—tail carriage faulty and flat feet.

Lacking stop and bumpy topskull with wide-set ears, short heavy muzzle, upright shoulders, narrow front and toes out, sloping topline to weak narrow rear, long back.

Ewe-necked, extremely upright shoulders, high withers with dip behind them, very straight behind and steep in the croup. Tail between legs indicates fear and/or shyness which are highly inappropriate.

Domed topskull, short thick neck, loaded shoulders, wide front, toes turning in, low on leg, soft topline, high in the rear, lacking sufficient angulation behind.

Color: *Body* rich fawn to russet mahogany with black overlay. The coat is characteristically double pigmented wherein the tip of each fawn hair is blackened. Belgian Tervurens characteristically becomes darker with age. On mature males, this blackening is especially pronounced on the shoulders, back and rib section.

Blackening in patches is undesirable. Although allowance should be made for females and young males, absence of blackening in mature dogs is a serious fault. Washed out, predominant color, such as cream or gray is to be severely penalized.

Chest is normally black, but may be a mixture of black and gray. A single white patch is permitted on the chest, not to extend to the neck or breast. Face has a black mask and the ears are mostly black. A face with a complete absence of black is a serious fault. Frost or white on chin or muzzle is normal. The underparts of the body, tail, and breeches are cream, gray, or light beige. The tail typically has a darker or black tip. *Feet*—The tips of the toes may be white. Nail color may vary from black to transparent. Solid black, solid liver or any area of white except as specified on the chest, tips of the toes, chin and muzzle are disqualifications.

Gait: Lively and graceful, covering the maximum ground with minimum effort. Always in motion, seemingly never tiring, he shows ease of movement rather than hard driving action. He single tracks at a fast gait, the legs both front and rear converging toward the center line of gravity of the dog. Viewed from the side he exhibits full extension of both fore and hindquarters. The backline should remain firm and level, parallel to the line of motion. His natural tendency is to move in a circle, rather than a straight line. Padding, hackneying, weaving, crabbing and similar movement faults are to be penalized according to the degree which they interfere with the ability of the dog to work.

Temperament: In his relationship with humans he is observant and vigilant with strangers, but not apprehensive. He does not show fear or shyness. He does not show viciousness by unwarranted or unprovoked attack. He must be approachable, standing his ground and showing confidence to meet overtures without himself making them. With those he knows well, he is most affectionate and friendly, zealous for their attention and very possessive.

Disqualifications:
- Males under 23 inches or over 26.5 inches or females under 21 inches or over 24.5 inches.
- Hanging ears, as on a hound.
- Undershot teeth such that contact with the upper incisors is lost by two or more of the lower incisors.
- A cropped or stump tail.
- Solid black, solid liver or any area of white except as specified on the chest, tips of the toes, chin and muzzle.

Approved September 11, 1990
Effective October 30, 1990

BELGIAN TERVUREN

GETTING STARTED

Welcome to the excitement of preparing to select a Belgian Tervuren puppy. When you and your family have decided that the Belgian Tervuren is really the most suitable dog for you, you can locate a recommended breeder and make a careful choice.

Before you talk to a breeder, you have to know what you intend to do with your new companion. He should fit into your daily routine, now and in the years to come. Will you show your new Belgian Tervuren or enter him in obedience or herding trials, or do you simply desire a pet and companion?

The responsibilities you will have and the consequences of owning a dog should be considered before you choose and visit a breeder, as your Belgian Tervuren will rely completely on you for his entire lifetime. You have to be prepared for dog ownership and you have to realize the following:

- All family members should be enthusiastic about acquiring a puppy;
- Your children should regard the dog, under your supervision, as a playmate, not a plaything, and they should be capable of respecting the dog. They should also be instructed in how to handle him properly;
- Taking care of a dog—feeding him, walking him, educating him, grooming him, looking after him for a lifetime—will be a time-consuming commitment;
- Food, boarding, veterinary bills, etc., must be included in the family budget;
- When you go away on vacation, you have to take him with you or somebody has to look after him, whether a friend or a boarding facility.

Are you ready for a bright, curious bundle of energy otherwise known as a Tervuren puppy?

If all of these requirements do not present a problem, you can begin your search for a reputable breeder, but do not act impulsively. Do not let your choice of a breeder be determined by his proximity to your home, and do not buy the first puppy that licks your nose.

Advice on buying a Belgian Tervuren puppy can be given by a veterinarian or you can inquire at a local dog club or trainer. The best way to find a reputable breeder, however, is to contact the American Belgian Tervuren Club (ABTC) for a breeder referral. The ABTC's member breeders are upheld to a strict code of ethics in their breeding programs as they promise to always keep the breed's best interests foremost.

A caring, responsible breeder raises his litters in his home or private kennel. When viewing a litter, he will give you good advice and assistance, but help him by letting him know the sex of the puppy you want (dog or bitch) and the purpose for which you desire the dog, as a family pet or for showing, competition, training, working, etc.

A good breeder consistently produces healthy and sound dogs and also provides good after-sales service. A responsible breeder will show you the dam of the litter and also the sire if available. Their appearance and behavior will give you some idea of your

FINDING A QUALIFIED BREEDER

Before you begin your puppy search, ask your veterinarian and perhaps other breeders to refer you to someone they believe is reputable. Responsible breeders usually raise only one or two breeds of dog. Avoid any breeder who has several different breeds or has several litters at the same time. Dedicated breeders are usually involved with a breed or other dog club. Many participate in some sport or activity related to their breed. Just as you want to be assured of the breeder's qualifications, the breeder wants to be assured that you will make a worthy owner. Expect the breeder to interview you, asking questions about your goals for the pup, your experience with dogs and what kind of home you will provide.

puppy's mature appearance and temperament. The breeder will also explain to you how a pedigree is read and inform you about the bloodlines and the merits of the pups' parents and grandparents. Do not underestimate the importance of the ancestors' character and anatomical structure if you wish your puppy to grow up to be a high-quality adult Belgian Tervuren. However, you have to realize that you are fortunate when you can make your puppy, coming from champion lines, a champion but also that a champion, coming from parents of inferior value, would be a miracle!

Watch the behavior of the puppies together in the litter. Do

A good breeder has the best interests of the breed in mind and can dedicate the time and care to raising the pups right.

> **SIGNS OF A HEALTHY PUPPY**
> Healthy puppies are robust little fellows who are alert and active, sporting shiny coats and supple skin. They should not appear lethargic, bloated or pot-bellied, nor should they have flaky skin or runny or crusted eyes or noses. Their stools should be firm and well formed, with no evidence of blood or mucus.

not choose a shy or retiring puppy; he may grow up to be insecure or fearful, a possible occurrence in the Belgian Tervuren. On the other hand, very assertive puppies can develop into overly dominant adults. Try to select an outgoing, confident, alert puppy who seems bright and looks healthy, who is willing to play and who comes running towards you. A puppy should not be fearful about normal noises. He should not hide but rather show interest when you drop a metal object like a key or hit a metal pan with a spoon. You should not buy any puppy of the litter, even one that seems to behave normally, if most of them show fear or cannot be approached. Ideally, when entering the room with the litter, the pups should all approach you, jump on you and compete for your attention. An extroverted character will be an advantage for training as well as showing. Take into consideration, though, that pups sleep as much as 18 hours a day and that your visit might coincide with one of their many naps.

A young Tervuren should appear bright, alert and inquisitive.

A SECOND CHANCE

For those considering adding a Tervuren to their lives, consider a rescue dog. The American Belgian Tervuren Club runs a rescue scheme to help Tervurens in need of new homes. Dogs taken into rescue are usually adults, but for some families this is a better option than a new puppy. A look at the rescue section of the club's website, www.abtc.org, gives potential adopters a look at what rescue volunteers do and how to start the adoption process, including:

• List of national coordinators and regional rescue contacts
• Adoption guide that gives information about the breed, rescued Tervs in particular and the adoption procedure
• Adoption application to print and mail in (pre-approval is recommended)
• Contract, which adopters are required to sign upon finalization of the adoption
• Forms for those who would like to volunteer with Tervuren rescue or provide a foster home
• Information for those who need to surrender a Tervuren
• Guidelines for shelters who have a Tervuren in their care
• Information on how to donate to Tervuren rescue.

If you want to buy a show-quality Belgian Tervuren, it is rather difficult for the author to offer concrete advice on structure and conformation of the puppy you are looking at without seeing it firsthand. An experienced breeder should be able to guide you in your choice of a puppy, especially as early as six to eight weeks. Just remember that there are very few people who are experts in the Belgian Tervuren and even experts can be mistaken.

A good Belgian Tervuren puppy should have a firm and square body; the back or topline should already be firm and horizontal, with no dip or roach (arching); the legs, both front and rear, should be straight and parallel to each other, not bowed and not placed too close together

MALE OR FEMALE?

Males of most breeds tend to be larger than their female counterparts; the male Tervuren also carries more coat around the head and neck. While males in many breeds tend to be more dominant and territorial, in the Tervuren the male is often the more sensitive sex. The female tends to have a more confident air about her. Both sexes are equally capable of being trained for performance events. Both sexes are wonderful and versatile companions, adding much enjoyment to pet and competition households alike, so the choice is really a personal preference.

(should not have a cowhocked look); and the ears should be as small as possible and between 7 and 12 weeks already standing firmly upright.

Rely upon the breeder's discretion when selecting the Terv puppy best for your living situation.

Choose a pup that, rather than hopping, already is able to trot easily, with a parallel movement of the fore- and hindquarters while the topline remains firm and level.

Coat color is important in the Belgian Tervuren. The amount of black overlay that a Tervuren will have when mature is not easily predictable but is often evident shortly after birth. In a Tervuren pup, you have to look for an overall warm fawn-based color, which can be seen from about seven weeks. The black overlay then develops again at that time. At any age, the dark muzzle or mask should always be pronounced. Likewise, any white should be avoided in the Tervuren, except when, at most, confined to the toes and a small patch on the forechest.

Decide which sex you prefer. There are some specific differences. Males are physically more impressive. They carry a bit more coat and generally have a major shedding about once a year. Bitches are more feminine, smaller and less powerfully built. Normally they come into season every 6 months for 21 days at a time. At the beginning, the heat cycle is marked with a clear mucus-like discharge from the vagina. Very often, however, the bitch's frequent licking is noticed first. After about seven days, the discharge is bloody and can be copious; during the third week, the discharge eases up. During this period of the season, you will have to keep your bitch away from male dogs in order to prevent unwanted matings. Moreover, some people find that a bitch is easier to house-train than a male.

Nevertheless, none of these sex differences should be overemphasized. In fact, both sexes are highly trainable and remarkably dedicated to their owners. Neutering and spaying, which is recommended for dogs not to be shown or bred, will eliminate some of these sex-related differences and offer health benefits as well.

The best age to bring a puppy home is between seven and eight weeks, certainly not older than nine. The reason is that during the

socialization period (3 to 12 weeks), the pups should be handled by a wide variety of people, exposed to as many experiences as possible and have contact with other dogs, other animals and humans, without becoming stressed.

You should ask the breeder to show you the parents' registration documents from the AKC, certificates of championships or performance awards and health certificates. When you purchase a pup, you will need copies of the pup's health records, including worming and vaccination, pedigree, registration certificate and sales contract. A responsible and caring breeder will also give you a diet sheet and possibly some food for the pup's first meals in his new home. A good breeder

Meeting the litter and getting to know what's underneath those little balls of fluff is the fun part of the puppy-picking process.

MAKE A COMMITMENT

Dogs are most assuredly man's best friend, but they are also a lot of work. When you add a puppy to your family, you also are adding to your daily responsibilities for years to come. Dogs need more than just food, water and a place to sleep. They also require training (which can be ongoing throughout the lifetime of the dog), activity to keep them physically and mentally fit and hands-on attention every day, plus grooming and health-care. Your life as you now know it may well disappear! Are you prepared for such drastic changes?

Don't choose on cuteness alone. Choose an active puppy who is interested in getting to know you.

in itself. Breed research, breeder selection and puppy visitation are very important aspects of finding the puppy of your dreams. Beyond that, these things also lay the foundation for a successful future with your pup. Puppy personalities within each litter vary, from the shy and easygoing puppy to the one who is dominant and assertive, with most pups falling somewhere in between. By spending time with the puppies you will be able to recognize certain behaviors and what these behaviors indicate about each pup's temperament. Which type of pup will comple-ment your family dynamics is best determined by observing the puppies in action within their "pack." Your breeder's expertise and recommendations are so valuable. Although you may fall in love with a bold and brassy male, the breeder may suggest that

will offer his help throughout the dog's life and will want to keep in touch with the owners of his dogs.

THE CONFIDENT TERVUREN OWNER

By now you should understand what makes the Belgian Tervuren a most unique and special dog, one that may fit nicely into your family and lifestyle. If you have researched breeders, you should be able to recognize a knowledge-able and responsible Belgian Tervuren breeder who cares not only about his pups but also about what kind of owner you will be. If you have completed the final step in your journey, you have found a litter, or possibly two, of quality Belgian Tervuren pups.

A visit with the puppies and their breeder will be an education

TEMPERAMENT ABOVE ALL ELSE

Regardless of breed, a puppy's disposition is perhaps his most important quality. It is, after all, what makes a puppy lovable and "livable." If the puppy's parents or grandparents are known to be snappy or aggressive, the puppy is likely to inherit those tendencies. That can lead to serious problems, such as the dog's becoming a biter, which can lead to eventual abandonment.

HEALTH MATTERS

When buying a puppy, one of the most important things to discuss with the breeder is health: the health of the breeder's line in general and specifically the health of the parents of the litter. American Belgian Tervuren Club members sign a Code of Ethics in which, among other things, they agree to learn about the breed and its health concerns, to be honest about their dogs' health and genetic backgrounds and to use their knowledge about genetic issues and breeding to produce "healthy, sound, quality" Tervurens.

Further, the health committee of the ABTC encourages its member breeders to ensure the health of their breeding animals through health screening with the Orthopedic Foundation for Animals (OFA) and the Canine Eye Registration Foundation (CERF). Tervurens are often screened and listed on the OFA registry for hips (dogs 24 months and older), elbows (24 months and older), cardiac disease (12 months and older) and thyroid disease (12 months and older, with periodic retesting throughout the dog's life at ages recommended by the OFA). CERF results are also listed in the OFA's database. CERF registers dogs that have been examined and declared free of genetic eye disease by members of the American College of Veterinary Ophthalmologists. Eye exams and recertification must be done on a yearly basis, as eye problems can arise at any time in a dog's life. For more information on these organizations, visit the OFA at www.offa.org and CERF at http://www.vmdb.org/cerf.html.

another pup would be best for you. The breeder's experience in rearing Belgian Tervuren pups and matching their temperaments with appropriate humans offers the best assurance that your pup will meet your needs and expectations. The type of puppy that you select is just as important as your decision that the Belgian Tervuren is the breed for you.

You know that the decision to live with a Belgian Tervuren is a serious commitment and not one to be taken lightly. This puppy is a living sentient being that will be dependent on you for basic survival for his entire life. Beyond the basics of survival—food, water,

shelter and protection—he needs much, much more. The new pup needs love, nurturing and a proper canine education to mold him into

It's not easy to select a puppy from a litter of healthy, happy and well-bred puppies, as one is as cute as the next!

a responsible, well-behaved canine citizen. Your Belgian Tervuren's health and good manners will need consistent monitoring and regular "tune-ups," so your job as a responsible dog owner will be ongoing throughout every stage of his life. If you are not prepared to accept these responsibilities and commit to them for at least the next decade, likely longer, then you are not prepared to own a dog of any breed.

Although the responsibilities of owning a dog may at times tax your patience, the joy of living with your Belgian Tervuren far outweighs the workload, and a well-mannered adult dog is well worth your time and effort. Before your very eyes, your new charge will grow up to be your most loyal friend, devoted to you unconditionally.

YOUR TERVUREN PUPPY SHOPPING LIST

Just as expectant parents prepare a nursery for their baby, so should you ready your home for the arrival of your Belgian Tervuren pup. If you have the necessary puppy supplies purchased and in place before he comes home, it will ease the puppy's transition from the warmth and familiarity of his mom and littermates to the brand-new environment of his new home and human family. You will be too busy to stock up and prepare your house after your pup comes home, that's for sure!

Your puppy's world presents many exciting challenges and new experiences. He will need boundaries and a watchful eye to keep him out of danger.

Imagine how a pup must feel upon being transported to a strange new place. It's up to you to comfort him and to let your little pup know that he is going to be happy with you.

FOOD AND WATER BOWLS

Your puppy will need separate bowls for his food and water. Stainless steel pans are generally preferred over plastic bowls since they sterilize better and pups are less inclined to chew on the metal. Heavy-duty ceramic bowls are popular, but consider how often you will have to pick up those heavy bowls. Buy adult-sized pans, as your puppy will grow into them quickly.

THE DOG CRATE

If you think that crates are tools of punishment and confinement for when a dog has misbehaved, think again. Most breeders and almost all trainers recommend a crate as the preferred house-training aid as well as for all-around puppy training and safety. Because dogs are natural den creatures that prefer cave-like environments, the benefits of crate use are many. The crate provides the puppy with his very own "safe house," a cozy place to sleep, take a break or seek comfort with a favorite toy; a travel aid to house your dog when on the road, at motels or at the vet's office; a training aid to help teach your puppy proper toileting habits; and

If you intend on taking your Terv puppy with you on excursions, a sturdy fiberglass crate is the safest mode.

When you can supervise the puppy, leave his crate door open so he can wander in and out of the crate as he chooses.

Along with your puppy comes a set of chomping puppy teeth! Encourage proper and safe chewing habits from the first day with your pup.

they are very lightweight and fold up into slim-line suitcases. However, a mesh crate might not be suitable for a pup with manic chewing habits or for an adult the size of the Tervuren.

Don't bother with a puppy-sized crate. Although your Belgian Tervuren will be fairly small when you bring him home, he will grow up in the blink of an eye and your puppy crate will be useless. Purchase a crate that will accommodate an adult Belgian Tervuren. He will stand up to about 25 inches at the withers when fully grown, so a large-sized

a place of solitude when non-dog people happen to drop by and don't want a lively puppy—or even a well-behaved adult dog—saying hello or begging for attention.

Crates come in several types, although the wire crate and the fiberglass airline-type crate are the most popular. Both are safe and your puppy will adjust to either one, so the choice is up to you. The wire crates offer better visibility for the pup as well as better ventilation. Many of the wire crates easily fold down into suitcase-size carriers. The fiberglass crates, similar to those used by the airlines for animal transport, are sturdier and more den-like. However, the fiberglass crates do not fold down and are less ventilated than a wire crate, which can be problematic in hot weather. Some of the newer crates are made of heavy plastic mesh;

crate will be necessary. Keep in mind that he will need to be able to fully stand, lie down and turn around comfortably.

BEDDING AND CRATE PADS

Your puppy will enjoy some type of soft bedding in his "room" (the crate), something he can snuggle into to feel cozy and secure. Old towels or blankets are good choices for a young pup, since he may (and probably will) have a toileting accident or two in the crate or decide to chew on the bedding material. Once he is fully trained and out of the early chewing stage, you can replace the puppy bedding with a permanent crate pad if you prefer. Crate pads and other dog beds run the gamut from inexpensive to high-end doggie-designer styles, but don't splurge on the good stuff until you are sure that your puppy is reliable and won't tear it up or make a mess on it.

PUPPY TOYS

Just as infants and older children require objects to stimulate their minds and bodies, puppies need toys to entertain their curious brains, wiggly paws and achy teeth. A fun array of safe doggie toys will help satisfy your puppy's chewing instincts and distract him from gnawing on the leg of your antique chair or your new leather sofa. Most puppy toys are cute and look as if they would

TOYS 'R SAFE

The vast array of tantalizing puppy toys is staggering. Stroll through any pet shop or pet-supply outlet and you will see that the choices can be overwhelming. However, not all dog toys are safe or sensible. Most very young puppies enjoy soft woolly toys that they can snuggle with and carry around. (You know they have outgrown them when they shred them up!) Avoid toys that have buttons, tabs or other enhancements that can be chewed off and swallowed. Soft toys that squeak are fun, but make sure your puppy does not disembowel the toy and remove (and swallow) the squeaker. Toys that rattle or make noise can excite a puppy, but they present the same danger as the squeaky kind and so require supervision. Hard rubber toys that bounce can also entertain a pup, but make sure that the toy is too big for your pup to swallow.

It is important to provide your Tervuren with chew toys, inside and out, so that he doesn't "have fun" with any of your valuables or ingest something that could harm him.

be a lot of fun, but not all are necessarily safe or good for your puppy, so use caution when you go puppy-toy shopping.

Although Belgian Tervuren are no more orally fixated than most other dogs, they certainly love to chew. The best "chewcifiers" are nylon and hard rubber bones, which are safe to gnaw on and come in sizes appropriate for all age groups and breeds. Be especially careful of natural bones, which can splinter or develop dangerous sharp edges; pups can easily swallow or choke on those bone splinters. Veterinarians often tell of surgical nightmares involving bits of splintered bone, because in addition to the danger of choking, the sharp pieces can damage the intestinal tract.

Similarly, rawhide chews, while a favorite of most dogs and puppies, can be equally dangerous. Pieces of rawhide are easily swallowed after they get soft and gummy from chewing,

and dogs have been known to choke on pieces of ingested rawhide. Rawhide chews should be offered only when you can supervise the puppy.

Soft woolly toys are special puppy favorites. They come in a wide variety of cute shapes and sizes; some look like little stuffed animals. Puppies love to shake them up and toss them about or simply carry them around. Be careful of fuzzy toys that have button eyes or noses that your pup could chew off and swallow, and make sure that he does not disembowel a squeaky toy to remove the squeaker. Braided rope toys are similar in that they are fun to chew and toss around, but they shred easily and the strings are easy to swallow. The strings are not digestible and, if the puppy doesn't pass them in his stool, he could end up at the vet's office. As with rawhides, your puppy should be closely monitored with rope toys.

If you believe that your pup has ingested a piece of one of his toys, check his stools for the next couple of days to see if he passes anything when he defecates. At the same time, also watch for signs of intestinal distress. A call to your veterinarian might be in order to get his advice and be on the safe side.

COLLARS
A lightweight nylon collar is the best choice for a very young pup. Quick-click collars are easy to put

Collaring Our Canines

The standard flat collar with a buckle or a snap, in leather, nylon or cotton, is widely regarded as the everyday all-purpose collar. If the collar fits correctly, you should be able to fit two fingers between the collar and the dog's neck.

Leather Buckle Collars

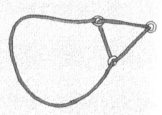

Limited-Slip Collar

Snap-Bolt Choke Collar

The martingale, Greyhound or limited-slip collar is preferred by many dog owners and trainers. It is fixed with an extra loop that tightens when pressure is applied to the leash. The martingale collar gets tighter but does not "choke" the dog. The limited-slip collar should only be used for walking and training, not for free play or interaction with another dog. These types of collar should never be left on the dog, as the extra loop can lead to accidents.

Choke collars, usually made of stainless steel, are made for training purposes but are not recommended for small dogs or heavily coated breeds. The chains can injure small dogs or damage long/abundant coats. Thin nylon choke leads are commonly used on show dogs while in the ring, though they are not practical for everyday use.

The harness, with two or three straps that attach over the dog's shoulders and around his torso, is a humane and safe alternative to the conventional collar. By and large, a well-made harness is virtually escape-proof. Harnesses are available in nylon and mesh and can be outfitted on most dogs, with chest girths ranging from 10 to 30 inches.

Harness

Nylon Collar

Quick-Click Closure

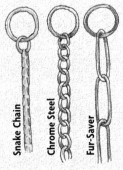

Snake Chain

Chrome Steel

Fur-Saver

Choke Chain Collars

A head collar, composed of a nylon strap that goes around the dog's muzzle and a second strap that wraps around his neck, offers the owner better control over his dog. This device is recommended for problem-solving with dogs (including jumping up, pulling and aggressive behaviors), but must be used with care.

A training halter, including a flat collar and two straps, made of nylon and webbing, is designed for walking. There are several on the market; some are more difficult to put on the dog than others. The halter harness, with two small slip rings at each end, is recommended for ease of use.

"See, look—it's not that bad." Your puppy must be acclimated to wearing a collar and lead as soon as you bring him home.

on and remove, and they can be adjusted as the puppy grows. Introduce him to his collar as soon as he comes home to get him accustomed to wearing it. He'll get used to it quickly and won't mind a bit. Make sure that it is snug enough that it won't slip off yet loose enough to be comfortable for the pup. You should be able to slip two fingers between the collar and his neck. Check the collar often, as puppies grow in spurts, and his collar can become too tight almost overnight. Choke collars are for training purposes only and should never be used on a puppy. Many trainers recommend head collars for the adult dog instead, and these humane devices are worth exploring, especially if your dog proves more difficult to train.

LEASHES

A 6-foot nylon lead is an excellent choice for a young puppy. It is lightweight and not as tempting to chew as a leather lead. You can switch to a 6-foot leather lead after your pup has grown and is used to walking politely on a lead. For initial puppy walks and house-training purposes, you should invest in a shorter lead so that you have more control over the puppy. At first you don't want him wandering too far away from you, and when taking him out for toileting you will want to keep him in the specific area chosen for his potty spot.

Once the puppy is heel-trained with a traditional leash, you can consider purchasing a retractable lead. A retractable lead is excellent for walking adult dogs that are already leash-wise. Provided you are strong enough to handle your Tervuren and get a retractable lead that can accommodate his weight, this type of lead is good for allowing the dog to roam farther away from you and explore a wider area when out walking, and it also retracts when you need to keep him close to you.

LEASH LIFE

Dogs love leashes! Believe it or not, most dogs dance for joy every time their owners pick up their leashes. The leash means that the dog is going for a walk—and there are few things more exciting than that! Here are some of the kinds of leashes that are commercially available.

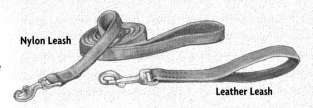

Nylon Leash

Leather Leash

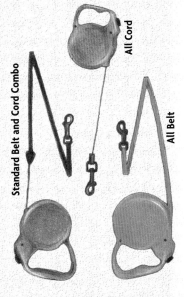

Standard Belt and Cord Combo

All Cord

All Belt

Retractable Leashes

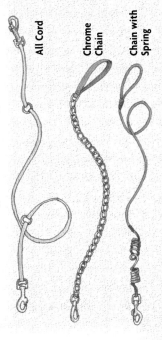

All Cord

Chrome Chain

Chain with Spring

Traditional Leash: Made of cotton, nylon or leather, these leashes are usually about 6 feet in length. A quality-made leather leash is softer on the hands than a nylon one. Durable woven cotton is a popular option. Lengths can vary up to about 48 feet, designed for different uses.

Chain Leash: Usually a metal chain leash with a plastic handle. This is not the best choice for most breeds, as it is heavier than other leashes and difficult to manage.

Retractable Leash: A long nylon cord is housed in a plastic device for extending and retracting. This leash, also known as a flexible leash, is ideal for taking trained dogs for long walks in open areas, although it is not always suitable for large, powerful breeds. Different lengths and sizes are available, so check that you purchase one appropriate for your dog's weight.

Elastic Leash: A nylon leash with an elastic extension. This is useful for well-trained dogs, especially in conjunction with a head halter.

Avoid leashes that are completely elastic, as they afford minimal control to the handler.

Adjustable Leash: This has two snaps, one on each end, and several metal rings. It is handy if you need to tether your dog temporarily, but is never to be used with a choke collar.

Tab Leash: A short leash (4 to 6 inches long) that attaches to your dog's collar. This device serves like a handle, in case you have to grab your dog while he's exercising off lead. It's ideal for "half-trained" dogs or dogs that listen only half of the time.

Slip Leash: Essentially a leash with a collar built in, similar to what a dog-show handler uses to show a dog. This British-style collar has a ring on the end so that you can form a slip collar. Useful if you have to catch your own runaway dog or a stray.

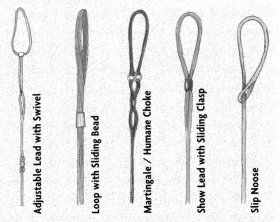

Adjustable Lead with Swivel

Loop with Sliding Bead

Martingale / Humane Choke

Show Lead with Sliding Clasp

Slip Noose

A Variety of Collar- and Leash-in-One Products

A Dog-Safe Home

The dog-safety police are taking you on a house tour. Let's go room by room and see how safe your own home is for your Tervuren pup. The following items are doggy dangers, so either they must be removed or the dog should be monitored or not allowed access to these areas.

Living Room

- house plants (some varieties are poisonous)
- fireplace or wood-burning stove
- paint on the walls (lead-based paint is toxic)
- lead drapery weights (toxic lead)
- lamps and electrical cords
- carpet cleaners or deodorizers

Outdoors

- swimming pool
- pesticides
- toxic plants
- lawn fertilizers

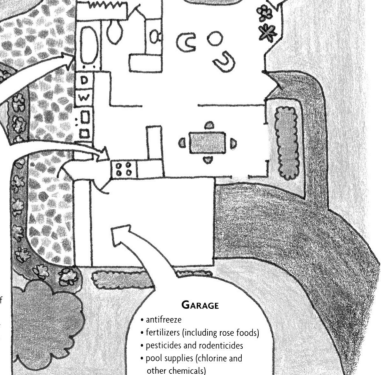

Bathroom

- blue water in the toilet bowl
- medicine cabinet (filled with potentially deadly bottles)
- soap bars, bleach, drain cleaners, etc.
- tampons

Kitchen

- household cleaners in the kitchen cabinets
- glass jars and canisters
- sharp objects (like kitchen knives, scissors and forks)
- garbage can (with remnants of good-smelling things like onions, potato skins, apple or pear cores, peach pits, coffee beans and other harmful tidbits)
- food left out on counters (some foods are toxic to dogs)

Garage

- antifreeze
- fertilizers (including rose foods)
- pesticides and rodenticides
- pool supplies (chlorine and other chemicals)
- oil and gasoline in containers
- sharp objects, electrical cords and power tools

HOME SAFETY FOR YOUR TERVUREN PUPPY

The importance of puppy-proofing cannot be overstated. In addition to making your house comfortable for your Belgian Tervuren's arrival, you also must make sure that your house is safe for your puppy before you bring him home. There are countless hazards in the owner's personal living environment that a pup can sniff, chew, swallow or destroy. Many are obvious; others are not. Do a thorough advance house check to remove or rearrange those things that could hurt your puppy, keeping any potentially dangerous items out of areas to which he will have access.

Electrical cords are especially dangerous, since puppies view them as irresistible chew toys. Unplug and remove all exposed cords or fasten them beneath baseboards where the puppy cannot reach them. Veterinarians and firefighters can tell you horror stories about electrical burns and house fires that resulted from puppy-chewed electrical cords. Consider this a most serious precaution for your puppy and the rest of your family.

Scout your home for tiny objects that might be seen at a pup's eye level. Keep medication bottles and cleaning supplies well out of reach, and do the same with waste baskets and other trash containers. It goes without saying that you should not use rodent

TOXIC PLANTS

Plants are natural puppy magnets, but many can be harmful, even fatal, if ingested by a puppy or adult dog. Scout your yard and home interior and remove any plants, bushes or flowers that could be even mildly dangerous. It could save your puppy's life. You can obtain a complete list of toxic plants from your veterinarian, at the public library or by looking online.

poison or other toxic chemicals in any puppy area and that you must keep such containers safely locked up. You will be amazed at how many places a curious puppy can discover!

Once your house has cleared inspection, check your yard. A sturdy fence, well embedded into the ground, will give your dog a safe place to play and potty. Although Belgian Tervurens are not known to be climbers or fence jumpers, they are incredibly athletic dogs, so at least a 6-foot-high fence will be necessary to

Tervurens are
naturally friendly
toward young
people, especially
when socialized
with children as
puppies.

Tervurens are naturally friendly toward young people, especially when socialized with children as puppies.

contain an agile youngster or adult. Check the fence periodically for necessary repairs. If there is a weak link or space to squeeze through, you can be sure a determined Belgian Tervuren will discover it.

The garage and shed can be hazardous places for a pup, as things like fertilizers, chemicals and tools are usually kept there. It's best to keep these areas off-limits to the pup. Antifreeze is especially dangerous to dogs, as they find the taste appealing and it takes only a few licks from the driveway to kill a dog, puppy or adult, small breed or large.

VISITING THE VETERINARIAN

A good vet is your Belgian Tervuren puppy's best health-insurance policy. If you do not already have a vet, ask friends and experienced dog people in your area for recommendations so that you can select a vet before you bring your Tervuren puppy home. Also arrange for your puppy's first veterinary examination before-hand, since many vets do not have appointments available immediately and your puppy should visit the vet within a day or so of coming home.

It's important to make sure your puppy's first visit to the vet is a pleasant and positive one. The vet should take great care to meet the pup and handle him gently to make their first meeting a positive experience. The vet will give the pup a thorough physical examination and set up a schedule for vaccinations and other necessary wellness visits. Be sure to show your vet any health and inoculation records, which you should have received from your breeder. Your vet is a great source of canine health information, so be sure to ask questions and take notes. Creating a health journal for your puppy will make a handy reference for his wellness and any future health problems that may arise.

MEETING THE FAMILY

Your Belgian Tervuren's homecoming is an exciting time for all members of the family, and it's only natural that everyone will be eager to meet him, pet him and play with him. However, for the puppy's sake, it's best to make these initial family meetings as uneventful as possible so that the pup is not overwhelmed with too much too soon. Remember, he has just left his dam and his litter-mates and is away from the breeder's home for the first time. Despite his wagging tail, he is still apprehensive and wondering where he is and who all these strange humans are. It's best to let him explore on his own and meet the family members as he feels comfortable. Let him investigate all the new smells, sights and sounds at his own pace. Children

should be especially careful to not get overly excited, use loud voices or hug the pup too tightly. Be calm, gentle and affectionate, and be ready to comfort him if he appears frightened or uneasy.

Be sure to show your puppy his new crate during his first day home. Toss a treat or two inside the crate; if he associates the crate with food, he will associate the crate with good things.

Your puppy may feel like a stranger in a strange land upon arrival at his new home. Don't worry, allow him to adapt at his own pace, and he will become one of the family.

FIRST NIGHT IN HIS NEW HOME

So much has happened in your Belgian Tervuren puppy's first day away from the breeder. He's had his first car ride to his new home. He's met his new human family and perhaps the other family pets. He has explored his new house and yard, at least those places where he is to be allowed during his first weeks at home. He may have visited his new veterinarian. He has eaten his first meal or two away from his dam and littermates.

Socialization—that is, introducing your pup around the neighborhood—will bring him out of his shell and make him a confident young dog, typical of the breed.

Surely that's enough to tire out an eight-week-old Belgian Tervuren pup—or so you hope!

It's bedtime. During the day, the pup investigated his crate, which is his new den and sleeping space, so it is not entirely strange to him. Line the crate with a soft towel or blanket that he can snuggle into and gently place him into the crate for the night. Some breeders send home a piece of bedding from where the pup slept with his littermates, and those familiar scents are a great comfort for the puppy on his first night without his siblings.

He will probably whine or cry. The puppy is objecting to the confinement and the fact that he is alone for the first time. This can be a stressful time for you as well as for the pup. It's important that you remain strong and don't let the puppy out of his crate to comfort him. He will fall asleep eventually. If you release him, the puppy will learn that crying means "out" and will continue that habit. You are laying the groundwork for future habits. Some breeders find that soft music can soothe a crying pup and help him get to sleep.

THE FAMILY FELINE

A resident cat has feline squatter's rights. The cat will treat the newcomer (your puppy) as she sees fit, regardless of what you do or say. So it's best to let the two of them work things out on their own terms. Cats have a height advantage and will generally leap to higher ground to avoid direct contact with a rambunctious pup. Some will hiss and boldly swat at a pup who passes by or tries to reach them. Keep the puppy under control in the presence of the cat to help them become accustomed to each other.

The relationship between a Tervuren and a cat or other household pet depends largely on the individual animals. Many, but not all, Tervs coexist peacefully with cats and/or other animals. It helps if the two have been raised together from their youth. Keep in mind that small animals or animals that run away from him may incite your Terv's chase instinct, which will be problematic.

SOCIALIZING YOUR PUPPY

The first 20 weeks of your Belgian Tervuren puppy's life are the most important of his entire lifetime. A properly socialized puppy will grow up to be a confident and stable adult who will be a pleasure to live with and a welcome addition to the neighborhood. The importance of socialization cannot be overemphasized. Research on canine behavior has proven that puppies who are not exposed to new sights, sounds, people and other animals during their first 20 weeks of life will grow up to be timid and fearful, even aggressive, and unable to flourish outside their familiar home environment.

Socializing your puppy is not difficult and, in fact, will be a fun time for you both. Lead training goes hand in hand with socialization, so your puppy will be learning how to walk on a lead at the same time that he's meeting the neighborhood. Because the Belgian Tervuren is such a remarkable dog—and not just another German Shepherd in the neighborhood—everyone will enjoy meeting "the new kid on the block." Take him for short walks to the park and to other dog-friendly places where he will encounter new people, especially children. Puppies automatically recognize children as "little people" and are drawn to play with them. Just make sure that

you supervise these meetings and that the children do not get too rough or encourage him to play too hard. An overzealous pup can often nip too hard, frightening the child and in turn making the puppy overly excited. A bad experience in puppyhood can impact a dog for life, so a pup that has a negative experience with a child may grow up to be shy or even aggressive around children.

Take your puppy along on your daily errands. Puppies are natural "people magnets," and most people who see your pup will want to pet him. All of these encounters will help to mold him into a confident adult dog. Likewise, you will soon feel like a confident, responsible dog owner, rightly proud of your well-mannered Tervuren.

New pet introductions should be done carefully, with you as a supervisor and facilitator.

Don't follow your pup's lead. Be the pack leader and let the puppy know that you are in charge and what you say is law.

socializing the puppy even before he has received all of his inoculations, depending on the individual puppy.

LEADER OF THE PUPPY'S PACK

Like other canines, your puppy needs an authority figure, someone he can look up to and regard as the leader of his "pack." His first pack leader was his dam, who taught him to be polite and not chew too hard on her ears or nip at her muzzle. He learned those same lessons from his litter-mates. If he played too rough, they cried in pain and stopped the game, which sent an important message to the rowdy puppy.

As puppies play together, they are also struggling to determine who will be the boss. Being pack

Be especially careful of your puppy's encounters and experiences during the eight-to-ten-week-old period, which is also called the "fear period." This is a serious imprinting period, and all contact during this time should be gentle and positive. A frightening or negative event could leave a permanent impression that could affect his future behavior if a similar situation arises.

Also make sure that your puppy has received his first and second rounds of vaccinations before you expose him to other dogs or bring him to places that other dogs may frequent. Avoid dog parks and other strange-dog areas until your vet assures you that your puppy is fully immunized and resistant to the diseases that can be passed between canines. Discuss socialization with your breeder, as some breeders recommend

KEEP OUT OF REACH

Most dogs don't browse around your medicine cabinet, but accidents do happen! The drug acetaminophen, the active ingredient in some pain killers, can be deadly to dogs and cats if ingested in large quantities. Acetaminophen toxicity, caused by the dog's swallowing 15 to 20 tablets, can be manifested in abdominal pains within a day or two of ingestion, as well as liver damage. If you suspect your dog has swiped a bottle of medicine, get the dog to the vet immediately so that the vet can induce vomiting and cleanse the dog's stomach.

animals, dogs need someone to be in charge. If a litter of puppies remained together beyond puppyhood, one of the pups would emerge as the strongest one, the one who calls the shots.

Once your puppy leaves the pack, he will look intuitively for a new leader. If he does not recognize you as that leader, he will try to assume that position for himself. Of course, it is hard to imagine your little Tervuren puppy trying to be in charge when he is so small and clueless. You must remember that these are natural canine instincts. Do not cave in and allow your pup to get the upper "paw."

Just as socialization is so important during these first 20 weeks, so too is your puppy's early education. He was born without any bad habits. He does not know what is good or bad behavior. If he does things like nipping and digging, it's because he is having fun and doesn't know that humans consider these things as "bad." It's your job to teach him good puppy manners, and this is the best time to accomplish that—before he has developed bad habits, since it is much more difficult to "unlearn" or correct unacceptable learned behavior than to teach good behavior from the start.

Make sure that all members of the family understand the importance of being consistent when training their new puppy. If

Who would think that these sweet babies could cause any mischief?

you tell the puppy to stay off the sofa and your daughter allows him to cuddle on the couch to watch her favorite television show, your pup will be confused about what he is and is not allowed to do. Have a family conference before your pup comes home so that everyone understands the basic principles of puppy training and the rules you have set forth for the pup, and agrees to follow them.

The old saying that "an ounce of prevention is worth a pound of cure" is especially true when it comes to puppies. It is much easier to prevent inappropriate behavior than it is to change it. It's also easier and less stressful for the pup, since it will keep discipline to a minimum and create a more positive learning environment for him. That, in turn, will also be easier on you.

Here are a few commonsense tips to keep your belongings safe and your puppy out of trouble:

- Keep your closet doors closed and your shoes, socks and other apparel off the floor so your puppy can't get at them.
- Keep a secure lid on the trash container or put the trash where your puppy can't dig into it. He can't damage what he can't reach.
- Supervise your puppy at all times to make sure he is not getting into mischief. If he starts to chew the corner of the rug, you can distract him instantly by tossing a toy for him to fetch. You also will be able to whisk him outside when you notice that he is about to piddle on the carpet. If you can't see your puppy, you can't teach him or correct his behavior.

Any inappropriate or undesired behavior from your pup must be consistently corrected by all members of the family, including the children.

SOLVING PUPPY PROBLEMS

CHEWING AND NIPPING

Nipping at fingers and toes is normal puppy behavior. Chewing is also the way that puppies investigate their surroundings. However, you will have to teach your puppy that chewing anything other than his toys is not acceptable. That won't happen overnight and at times puppy teeth will test your patience. However, if you allow nipping and chewing to continue, just think about the damage that a mature Belgian Tervuren can do with a full set of adult teeth. Have you ever seen a Tervuren biting the sleeve at a Schutzhund trial?

Whenever your puppy nips your hand or fingers, cry out "Ouch!" in a loud voice, which should startle your puppy and stop him from nipping, even if only for a moment. Immediately distract him by offering a small treat or an appropriate toy for him to chew instead (which means having chew toys and puppy treats handy or in your pockets at all times). Praise him when he takes the toy and tell him what a good fellow he is. Praise is far more important in puppy training than discipline and correction.

Puppies also tend to nip at children more often than adults, since they perceive little ones to be more vulnerable and more

similar to their littermates. Teach your children appropriate responses to nipping behavior. If they are unable to handle it themselves, you may have to intervene. Puppy nips can be quite painful and a child's frightened reaction will only encourage a puppy to nip harder, which is a natural canine response. As with all other puppy situations, interaction between your Belgian Tervuren puppy and children should be supervised.

Chewing on objects, not just family members' fingers and ankles, is also normal canine behavior that can be especially tedious (for the owner, not the pup) during the teething period when the puppy's adult teeth are coming in. At this stage, chewing just plain feels good. Furniture legs and cabinet corners are common puppy favorites. Shoes and other personal items also taste pretty good to a pup.

The best solution is, once again, prevention. If you value something, keep it tucked away and out of reach. You can't hide your dining-room table in a closet, but you can try to deflect the chewing by applying a bitter product made just to deter dogs from chewing. Available in a spray or cream, this substance is vile-tasting, although safe for dogs, and most puppies will avoid the forbidden object after one tiny taste. You also can

BE CONSISTENT
Consistency is a key element, in fact is absolutely necessary, to a puppy's learning environment. A behavior (such as chewing, jumping up or climbing onto the furniture) cannot be forbidden one day and then allowed the next. That will only confuse the pup, and he will not understand what he is supposed to do. Just one or two episodes of allowing an undesirable behavior to "slide" will imprint that behavior on a puppy's brain and make that behavior more difficult to erase or change.

apply the product to your leather leash if the puppy tries to chew on his lead during leash-training sessions.

Keep a ready supply of safe chews handy to offer your Belgian Tervuren as a distraction when he starts to chew on something that's a "no-no" and praise him when he chews on the acceptable items. Remember, at this tender age he does not yet know what is permitted or forbidden, so you have to be "on call" every minute he's awake and on the prowl.

You may lose a treasure or two during your puppy's growing-up period, and the furniture could sustain a nasty nick or two. These can be trying times, so be prepared for those inevitable accidents and comfort yourself in knowing that this too shall pass.

An alert, athletic and inquisitive breed like the Tervuren can get into all kinds of dangerous trouble if you do not take control and nip bad behavior in the bud.

JUMPING UP

Although Belgian Tervuren pups are not known to be notorious jumpers, they are still puppies after all, and puppies jump up— on you, your guests, your counters and your furniture. Just another normal part of growing up, and one you need to meet head-on before it becomes an ingrained habit.

The key to jump correction is consistency. You cannot correct your Belgian Tervuren for jumping up on you today, then allow it to happen tomorrow by greeting him with hugs and kisses. As you have learned by now, consistency is critical to all puppy lessons.

For starters, try turning your back as soon as the puppy jumps. Jumping up is a means of gaining your attention and, if the pup can't see your face, he may get discouraged and learn that he loses eye contact with his beloved master when he jumps up.

Leash corrections also work, and most puppies respond well to a leash tug if they jump. Grasp the leash close to the puppy's collar and give a quick tug downward, using the command "Off." Do not use the word "Down," since "Down" is used to teach the puppy to lie down, which is a separate action that he will learn during his education in the basic commands. As soon as the puppy has backed off, tell him to sit and immediately praise him for doing so. This will take many repetitions and won't be accomplished quickly, so don't get discouraged or give up; you must be even more persistent than your puppy.

A second method used for jump correction is the spritzer bottle. Fill a spray bottle with water mixed with a bit of lemon juice or vinegar. As soon as the puppy jumps, command him "Off" and spritz him with the water mixture. Of course, that means having the spray bottle handy whenever or wherever jumping usually happens.

Yet a third method to discourage jumping is grasping the puppy's paws and holding them gently but firmly until he struggles to get away. Wait a brief moment or two, then release his paws and give him a command to sit. He should eventually learn that jumping gets him into an uncomfortable predicament.

Children are major victims of puppy jumping, since puppies view little people as ready targets for jumping up as well as nipping. If your children (or their friends) are unable to dispense jump corrections, you will have to intervene and handle it for them.

Important to prevention is also knowing what you should *not* do. Never kick your Belgian Tervuren (for any reason, not just for jumping) or knock him in the chest with your knee. That maneuver could actually harm your puppy. Vets can tell you stories about puppies who suffered broken bones after being banged about when they jumped up.

PUPPY WHINING

Puppies often cry and whine, just as infants and little children do. It's their way of telling us that they are lonely or in need of attention. Your puppy will miss his littermates and will feel insecure when he is left alone. You may be out of the house or just in another room, but he will still feel alone. During these times, the puppy's crate should be his personal comfort station, a place all his own where he can feel safe and secure. Once he learns that being alone is okay

and not something to be feared, he will settle down without crying or objecting. You might want to leave a radio on while he is crated, as the sound of human voices can be soothing and will give the impression that people are around.

Give your puppy a favorite sturdy toy to entertain him whenever he is crated. You will both be happier: the puppy because he feels safe in his den and you because he is quiet, safe and not going on puppy escapades that can wreak havoc in your house or cause him danger.

To make sure that your puppy will always view his crate as a safe and cozy place, never, *ever* use the crate as punishment. That's the best way to turn the crate into a negative place that the pup will want to avoid. Sure, you can use the crate for your own peace of mind if your puppy is getting into trouble and needs some "time out." Just don't let him know that! Never scold the pup and immediately place him into the crate. Count to ten, give him a couple of hugs and maybe a treat, then scoot him into his crate.

It's also important not to make a big fuss when he is released from the crate. That will make getting out of the crate more appealing than being in the crate, which is just the opposite of what you are trying to achieve.

BELGIAN TERVUREN

You are what you eat! The same is true for your Terv pup. Feed a diet recommended by your veterinarian or breeder.

Adding a Belgian Tervuren to your household means adding a new family member who will need your care each and every day. When your Belgian Tervuren pup first comes home, you will start a routine with him so that, as he grows up, your dog will have a daily schedule just as you do. The aspects of your dog's daily care will likewise become regular parts of your day, so you'll both have a new schedule. Dogs learn by consistency and thrive on routine: regular times for meals, exercise, grooming and potty trips are just as important for your dog as they are for you! Your dog's schedule will depend much on your family's daily routine, but remember that you now have a new member of the family who is part of your day every day.

FEEDING

Feeding your dog the best diet is based on various factors, including age, activity level, overall condition and size of breed. When you visit the breeder, he will share with you his advice about the proper diet for your dog based on his experience with the breed and the foods with which he has had success. Likewise, your vet will be a helpful source of advice throughout the dog's life and will aid you in planning a diet for optimal health.

DIET DON'TS
- Got milk? Don't give it to your dog! Dogs cannot tolerate large quantities of cows' milk, as they do not have the enzymes to digest lactose.
- You may have heard of dog owners who add raw eggs to their dogs' food for a shiny coat or to make the food more palatable, but consumption of raw eggs too often can cause a deficiency of the vitamin biotin.
- Avoid feeding table scraps, as they will upset the balance of the dog's complete food. Additionally, fatty or highly seasoned foods can cause upset canine stomachs.
- Do not offer raw meat to your dog. Raw meat can contain parasites; it also is high in fat.
- Vitamin A toxicity in dogs can be caused by too much raw liver, especially if the dog already gets enough vitamin A in his balanced diet, which should be the case.
- Bones like chicken, pork chop and other soft bones are not suitable, as they easily splinter.

FEEDING THE PUPPY

Of course, your pup's very first food will be his dam's milk. There may be special situations in which pups fail to nurse, necessitating that the breeder hand-feed them with a formula, but for the most part pups spend the first weeks of life nursing from their dam. The breeder weans the pups by gradually introducing solid foods and decreasing the milk meals. Pups may even start themselves off on the weaning process, albeit inadvertently, if they snatch bites from their mom's food bowl. By the time the pups are ready for new homes, they are fully weaned and eating a good puppy food. As a new owner, you may be thinking, "Great! The breeder has taken care of the hard part." Not so fast.

A puppy's first year of life is the time when all or most of his growth and development takes place. This is a delicate time, and diet plays a huge role in proper skeletal and muscular formation. Improper diet and exercise habits can lead to damaging problems that will compromise the dog's health and movement for his entire life. That being said, new owners should not worry needlessly. With the myriad types of food formulated specifically for growing pups of different-sized breeds, dog-food manufacturers have taken much of the guesswork out of feeding your puppy well. Since growth-food formulas are designed to provide the nutrition that a growing puppy needs, it is unnecessary and, in fact, can prove harmful to add supplements to the diet. Research has shown that too much of certain vitamin supplements and minerals predispose a dog to skeletal problems. It's by no means a case of "if a little is good, a lot is better." At every stage of

Pups get the best start in life from nursing from their mother. It's hard work being mom to a hungry litter.

Pups get the best start in life from nursing from their mother. It's hard work being mom to a hungry litter.

your dog's life, too much or too little in the way of nutrients can be harmful, which is why a manufactured complete food is the easiest way to know that your dog is getting what he needs.

Because of a young pup's small body and accordingly small digestive system, his daily portion will be divided up into small meals throughout the day. This can mean starting off with three or more meals a day and decreasing the number of meals as the pup matures. For the adult, dividing the day's food into two meals on a morning/evening schedule is much healthier for the dog's digestion than feeding one large daily portion.

Regarding the feeding schedule, feeding the pup at the same times and in the same place each day is important for both housebreaking purposes and establishing the dog's everyday routine. As for the amount to feed, growing puppies generally need proportionately more food per body weight than their adult counterparts, but a pup should never be allowed to gain excess weight. Dogs of all ages should be kept in proper body condition, but extra weight can strain a pup's developing frame, causing skeletal problems.

Watch your pup's weight as he grows and, if the recommended amounts seem to be too much or too little for your pup, consult the vet about appropriate dietary changes. Keep in mind that treats, although small, can quickly add up throughout the day, contributing unnecessary calories. Treats are fine when used prudently; opt for dog treats specially formulated to be healthy or for nutritious snacks like small pieces of cheese or cooked chicken.

FEEDING THE ADULT DOG

For the adult (meaning physically mature) dog, feeding properly is about maintenance, not growth. Again, correct weight is a concern. Your dog should appear fit and should have an evident "waist." His ribs should not be protruding (a sign of being underweight), but they should be covered by only a slight layer of

fat. Under normal circumstances, an adult dog can be maintained fairly easily with a high-quality nutritionally complete adult-formula food.

Factor treats into your dog's overall daily caloric intake, and avoid offering table scraps. Not only are certain "people foods," like chocolate, onions, nuts, grapes and raisins, toxic to dogs but feeding table scraps encourages begging and overeating. Overweight dogs are more prone to health problems. Research has even shown that obesity takes years off a dog's life. With that in mind, resist the urge to overfeed and over-treat. Don't make unnecessary additions to your dog's diet, whether with tidbits or with extra vitamins and minerals.

The amount of food needed for proper maintenance will vary

It is vital that your Tervuren's diet be balanced. Treats count, too, and a balanced diet can easily be "unbalanced" by too many extras.

NOT HUNGRY?

No dog in his right mind would turn down his dinner, would he? If you notice that your dog has lost interest in his food, there could be any number of causes. Dental problems are a common cause of appetite loss, one that is often overlooked. If your dog has a toothache, a loose tooth or sore gums from infection, chances are it doesn't feel so good to chew. Think about when you've had a toothache! If your dog does not approach the food bowl with his usual enthusiasm, look inside his mouth for signs of a problem. Whatever the cause, you'll want to consult your vet so that your chow hound can get back to his happy, hungry self as soon as possible.

Your Tervuren's diet will be based on the dog's age and activity level. The breed remains active into double digits.

depending on the individual dog's activity level, but you will be able to tell whether the daily portions are keeping him in good shape. With the wide variety of good complete foods available, choosing what to feed is largely a matter of personal preference. Just as with the puppy, the adult dog should have consistency in his mealtimes and feeding place. In addition to a consistent routine, regular mealtimes also allow the owner to see how much his dog is eating. If the dog seems never to be satisfied or, likewise, becomes uninterested in his food, the owner will know right away that something is wrong and can consult the vet.

Keep in mind, also, that your very active Tervuren may require more food than you might expect. The more a dog does, the more he needs to eat! Examples of dogs with higher nutrient requirements are dogs who are very active in training for or competing in sporting disciplines and dogs that are used in a working capacity such as herding or hunting. They do not need supplementation to their regular food; rather, because they need larger amounts of all nutrients, they will need their maintenance food in larger portions. Also ask your vet about specially formulated "performance" diets for active dogs.

When feeding an active dog, it is essential to provide adequate periods of rest (an hour or more) before and after eating to avoid stomach upset or the more serious gastric torsion, which can be fatal. Treats can be fed during rest periods to keep up the dog's energy in between meals, and water can be offered as well (but remember—no gulping!). The dog needs time to settle down before and after any eating or drinking, so breaks should be factored into the training program or work routine. Be sure to discuss bloat with your vet so that you know what precautions to take every day to protect your Tervuren and also so you can recognize symptoms, as a dog needs *immediate* veterinary attention if signs of bloat occur. It's a matter of life and death for an affected dog.

DIETS FOR THE AGING DOG

A good rule of thumb is that once a dog has reached about 75% of his expected lifespan, he has reached "senior citizen" or geriatric status. Your Belgian Tervuren will be considered a senior at about 8 years of age; based on his size, he has a projected lifespan of about 12 to 14 years.

What does aging have to do with your dog's diet? He will require some dietary changes to accommodate the changes that come along with increased age. One change is that the older dog's dietary needs become more similar to those of a puppy. Specifically, dogs can metabolize more protein as youngsters and seniors than in the adult-maintenance stage. Discuss with your vet whether you need to switch to a higher-protein or senior-formulated food or whether your current adult-dog food contains sufficient nutrition for the senior.

Watching the dog's weight remains essential, even more so in the senior stage. Older dogs are already more vulnerable to illness, and obesity only contributes to their susceptibility to problems. As the older dog becomes less active and thus exercises less, his regular portions may cause him to gain weight. At this point, you may consider decreasing his daily food intake or switching to a reduced-calorie food. As with other changes, you should consult your vet for advice.

TYPES OF FOOD AND READING THE LABEL

When selecting the type of food to feed your dog, it is important to check out the label for ingredients. Many dry-food products have soybean, corn or rice as the main ingredient. The main ingredient will be listed first on the label, with the rest of the ingredients following in descending order according to their proportion in the food. While these types of dry food are acceptable, you really should look into dry foods based on meat or fish. These are better-quality foods and thus higher priced.

HOLD THE ONIONS

Sliced, chopped or grated; dehydrated, boiled, fried or raw; or pearl, Spanish, white or red: onions can be deadly to your dog. The toxic effects of onions in dogs are cumulative for up to 30 days. A serious form of anemia, called Heinz body anemia, affects the red blood cells of dogs that have eaten onions. For safety (and better breath), dogs should avoid chives and scallions as well.

However, they may be just as economical in the long run, because studies have shown that it takes less of the higher-quality foods to maintain a dog.

Comparing the various types of food, dry, canned and semi-moist, dry foods contain the least amount of water and canned foods the most. Proportionately, dry foods are the most calorie- and nutrient-dense, which means that you need more of a canned food product to supply the same amount of nutrition. In households with breeds of different sizes, the canned/dry/semi-moist question can be of special importance. Larger breeds obviously eat more than smaller ones and thus in general do better on dry foods, but smaller breeds do fine on canned foods and require "small bite" formulations to protect their small mouths and teeth if fed dry foods. So if you have breeds of different sizes in your home, consider both your own preferences and what your dogs like to eat, but in general think canned for the little guys and dry or semi-moist for everyone else. You may find success mixing the food types as well. Water is important for all dogs, but even more so for those fed dry foods, as there is no high water content in their food.

There are strict controls that regulate the nutritional content of dog food, and a food has to meet the minimum requirements in order to be considered "complete and balanced." It is important that you choose such a food for your dog, so check the label to be sure that your chosen food meets the requirements. If not, look for a food that clearly states on the label that it is formulated to be complete and balanced for your dog's partic-ular stage of life.

Recommendations for amounts to feed will also be indicated on the label. You should also ask your vet about proper food portions, and you will need to keep an eye on your dog's condition to see whether the recommended amounts are adequate. If he becomes over- or underweight, you will need to make adjustments; this also would be a good time to consult your vet.

The food label may also make feeding suggestions, such as whether moistening a dry-food product is recommended. Sometimes a splash of water will make the food more palatable for the dog and even enhance the flavor. Don't be overwhelmed by the many factors that go into feeding your dog. Manufacturers of complete and balanced foods make it easy, and once you find the right food and amounts for your Belgian Tervuren, his daily feeding will be a matter of routine.

DON'T FORGET THE WATER

For a dog, it's always time for a drink! Regardless of what type of food he eats, there's no doubt that he needs plenty of water. Fresh cold water, in a clean bowl, should be freely available to your dog at all times. There are special circumstances, such as during puppy housebreaking, when you will want to monitor your pup's water intake so that you will be able to predict when he will need to relieve himself, but water must be available to him nonetheless. Water is essential for hydration and proper body function just as it is in humans.

You will get to know how much your dog typically drinks in a day. Of course, in the heat or if exercising vigorously, he will be more thirsty and will drink more. However, if he begins to drink noticeably more water for no apparent reason, this could signal any of various problems, and you are advised to consult your vet.

Water is the best drink for dogs. Some owners are tempted to give milk from time to time or to moisten dry food with milk, but dogs do not have the enzymes necessary to digest the lactose in milk, which is much different than the milk that nursing puppies receive. Therefore, stick with clean fresh water to quench your dog's thirst, and always have it readily available to him.

A word of caution concerning your deep-chested Tervuren's water intake: he should never be allowed to gulp water, especially at mealtimes. In fact, his water intake should be limited at mealtimes as a rule. This simple daily precaution can go a long way in protecting your dog from the dangerous and potentially fatal gastric torsion (bloat).

EXERCISE

The Belgian Tervuren thrives on physical stimulation and activity. Owners who cannot offer their dogs abundant

QUENCHING HIS THIRST

Is your dog drinking more than normal and trying to lap up everything in sight? Excessive drinking has many different causes. Obvious causes for a dog's being thirstier than usual are hot weather and vigorous exercise. However, if your dog is drinking more for no apparent reason, you could have cause for concern. Serious conditions like kidney or liver disease, diabetes and various types of hormonal problems can all be indicated by excessive drinking. If you notice your dog's being excessively thirsty, contact your vet at once. Hopefully there will be a simpler explanation, but the earlier a serious problem is detected, the sooner it can be treated, with a better rate of cure.

A Tervuren working or playing is poetry in motion, and exercise like this is an absolute necessity for this active herding breed.

reliably when you call him to return to you. Since the breed was designed to run and work vigorously from sunrise to sunset, it is no mystery why this majestic athlete needs a couple of hours of daily invigorating activity to keep fit physically and mentally. Remember, a well-exercised Belgian Tervuren is a happy one, and a happy dog is so much easier to train, live with and love.

Remember that some precautions should be taken with a puppy's exercise. During his first year, when he is growing and developing, your Belgian Tervuren should not be subject to too-vigorous activity that stresses his body. Short walks at a comfortable pace and play sessions in the yard are good for a growing pup, and his exercise can be increased as he grows up.

exercise will not enjoy the company of inactive Belgian Tervurens. A sedentary lifestyle is very harmful to this breed, and the dog can adopt many unacceptable behaviors if he is not properly exercised.

Few breeds are as talented as the Belgian Tervuren, and its physical abilities are boundless. Your Belgian will welcome daily walks on a loose or retractable lead. Free running is the best type of exercise for your dog, but never allow your Belgian off lead unless you are in an enclosed field, fenced area or some other safe area. The beach or an open field can be good locations for the Belgian Tervuren to release his pent-up energy and spirit, but always be aware of the local laws before letting your dog exercise in a public place. You must have total control of your Tervuren, and he must *always* respond

PUPPY STEPS
Puppies are brimming with activity and enthusiasm. It seems that they can play all day and night without tiring, but don't overdo your puppy's exercise regimen. Easy does it for the puppy's first six to nine months. Keep walks brief and don't let the puppy engage in stressful jumping games. The puppy frame is delicate, and too much exercise during those critical growing months can cause injury to his bone structure, ligaments and musculature. Save his first jog for his first birthday!

Selecting the Right Brushes and Combs

Will a rubber curry make my dog look slicker? Is a rake smaller than a pin brush? Do I choose nylon or natural bristles? Buying a dog brush can make the hairs on your head stand on end! Here's a quick once-over to educate you on the different types of brushes.

Slicker Brush: Fine metal prongs closely set on a curved base. Used to remove dead coat from the undercoat of medium- to long-coated breeds.

Pin Brush: Metal pins, often covered with rubber tips, set on an oval base. Used to remove shedding hair and is gentler than a slicker brush.

Metal Comb: Steel teeth attached to a steel handle; the closeness and size of the teeth vary greatly. A "flea comb" has tiny teeth set very closely together and is used to find fleas in a dog's coat. Combs with wider teeth are used for detangling longer coats.

Rake: Long-toothed comb with a short handle. Used to remove undercoat from heavily coated breeds with dense undercoats.

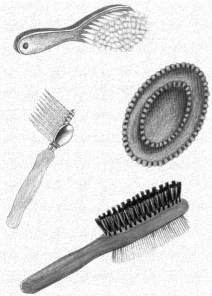

Soft-bristle Brush: Nylon or natural bristles set in a plastic or wood base. Used on short coats or long coats (without undercoats).

Rubber Curry: Rubber prongs, with or without a handle. Used for short-coated dogs. Good for use during shampooing.

Combination Brushes: Two-sided brush with a different type of bristle on each side; for example, pin brush on one side and slicker on the other, or bristle brush on one side and pin brush on the other. An economical choice if you need two kinds of brushes.

Grooming Glove: Sometimes called a hound glove; used to give sleek-coated dogs a once-over.

Brushing the coat daily will stimulate the coat's natural oils, remove dead hair and prevent matting.

your dog every day, continually strengthening the bond between the two of you. Furthermore, exercising together will improve health and longevity for both of you. You both need exercise, and now you and your dog have a workout partner and motivator!

GROOMING THE BELGIAN TERVUREN

MAINTAINING THE COAT

Whether you plan to show your Tervuren or if he is simply a companion dog, you will need to do some routine grooming on your dog. Unlike his shorthaired Malinois brother, the Tervuren is a long-coated dog that will require weekly grooming. Your Tervuren will have an outer coat with long, straight, abundant guard hairs, and he will also have a very dense undercoat, which will protect him in all weather conditions. Around his neck he will have a mane of fur, and he will have longer hairs, like a fringe, on his front legs. His tail will have a heavy feathering of fur. A Tervuren who is in top condition will have an overlay of black hairs over his basic coat color; this is a beautiful sight. A well-maintained Tervuren will be striking with his gleaming coat of rich color!

For overweight dogs, dietary changes and activity will help the goal of weight loss. While they should be encouraged to be active, remember not to overdo it, as the excess weight is already putting strain on his vital organs and bones. As for highly active dogs, some of them never seem to tire. They will enjoy time spent with their owners doing things together.

Regardless of your dog's condition and activity level, exercise offers benefits to all dogs and owners. Consider the fact that dogs who are kept active are more stimulated both physically and mentally, meaning that they are less likely to become bored and lapse into destructive behavior. Also consider the benefits of one-on-one time with

Start grooming your puppy within a week of bringing him home. This will give you a good start in getting him used to grooming time. The benefits of regular grooming include more than just a healthy coat. Grooming time is essential owner-dog bonding time, building the dog's trust in you, his owner. It also is time that you spend working up close and hands-on with your dog, allowing you to check for any abnormalities that may signal a health problem. You may work with him on a table while he is still young and relatively small or perhaps groom him on the floor, either with him standing or lying on a blanket. As his size increases, you may prefer to put him on a grooming table.

You will need some grooming tools, which can be purchased at your local pet-supply shop. You should have a slicker brush, a pin brush, a metal comb with medium-spaced teeth for combing through mats or combing out dead hair, a good pair of scissors, thinning shears and a spray bottle. Your Tervuren should be brushed out once a week. With regular weekly grooming, your Tervuren is not likely to need a bath more than a few times a year, as in addition to removing dirt from the coat, routine brushing keeps the coat shiny and healthy.

The grooming routine should be established as a basic ritual, always using the same technique. Your dog can be groomed when standing, but when he is acting strong-willed you should command him to lie down on his side. In this position it is also easier to reach certain parts of the body such as the stomach and the insides of the legs.

Begin by holding a section of hair open with your hand and then, following the lay of the coat, brush or comb the section below your hand. You continue this way until you have groomed the entire coat. You can use a softer brush on the belly and flanks. Your dog should be standing while you groom the back, neck, chest, legs and feet.

Thoroughly brush or comb through the feathery hair found behind the ears, on the rear sides of the legs, on the tail and inside the thighs to remove tangles or stray strands of hair. It is possible to work out tangles of hair with your fingers, always being careful not to hurt the dog. Flattening the coat on the body, using your comb or a glove made for this purpose, completes the routine grooming. This is the basic grooming procedure for either the pet Tervuren or the Terv in the show ring.

Your Belgian Tervuren will drop his coat once or twice a year, and at this time you should groom him on a daily basis to remove dead hair, prevent matting and see that a new and healthy coat emerges.

Acclimate your Tervuren to the grooming routine at a young age so he is comfortable with it as an adult.

BATHING

Your Tervuren does not need bathing more than every three or four months unless he gets into something messy or starts to smell like a dog. Show dogs may be bathed more frequently, although that depends on the owner. Bathing too frequently can have negative effects on the skin and coat, removing natural oils and causing dryness.

If you give your dog his first bath when he is young, he will become accustomed to the process. Wrestling a dog into the tub or chasing a freshly shampooed dog who has escaped from the bath will be no fun. Most dogs don't naturally enjoy their baths, but you at least want yours to cooperate with you.

Before bathing the dog, have the items you'll need close at hand. First, decide where you will bathe the dog. You should have a tub or basin with a non-slip surface. Small puppies can even be bathed in a sink. In warm weather, some people like to use a portable pool in the yard, although you'll want to make sure your dog doesn't head for the nearest dirt pile following his bath. You will also need a hose or shower spray to wet the coat thoroughly, a shampoo formulated for dogs, absorbent towels and perhaps a blow dryer. Human shampoos are too harsh for dogs' coats and will dry them out.

Before wetting the dog, give him a brush-through to remove any dead hair, dirt and mats. Make sure he is at ease in the tub and have the water at a comfortable temperature. Begin bathing by wetting the coat all the way down to the skin. Massage in the shampoo, keeping it away from his face and eyes. Rinse him thoroughly, again avoiding the eyes and ears, as you don't want to get water into the ear canals. A thorough rinsing is important, as shampoo residue is drying and itchy to the dog. After rinsing, wrap him in a towel to absorb the initial moisture. You can finish drying with either a towel or a blow dryer on low heat, held at a safe distance from the dog. You should keep the dog indoors and away from drafts until he is completely dry. Once his coat is dry, give him another thorough brushing.

NAIL CLIPPING

Having their nails trimmed is not on many dogs' lists of favorite things to do. With this in mind, you will need to accustom your puppy to the procedure at a young age so that he will sit still (well, as still as he can) for his pedicures. Long nails can cause the dog's feet to spread, which is not good for him; likewise, long nails can hurt if they unintentionally scratch, not good for you.

Some dogs' nails are worn down naturally by regular walking on hard surfaces, so the frequency with which you clip depends on your individual dog. Look at his nails from time to time and clip as needed; a good way to know when it's time for a trim is if you hear your dog clicking as he walks across the floor.

There are several types of nail clippers and even electric (or battery-operated) nail-grinding tools made for dogs; first we'll discuss using the clipper. To start, have your clipper ready and some doggie treats on hand. You want your pup to view his nail-clipping sessions in a positive light, and what better way to convince him than with food? You may want to

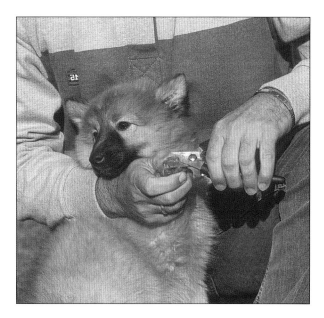

enlist the help of an assistant to comfort the pup and offer treats as you concentrate on the clipping itself. The guillotine-type clipper is thought of by many as the easiest type to use, though it may not be suitable for the Tervuren adult; the nail tip is inserted into the opening, and blades on the top and bottom snip it off in one clip.

Start by grasping the pup's paw; a little pressure on the foot pad causes the nail to extend, making it easier to clip. Clip off a little at a time. If you can see the "quick," which is a blood vessel that runs through each nail, you will know how much to trim, as you do not want to cut into the quick. On that note, if you do cut the quick, which will cause bleeding, you can stem the flow of

Special nail clippers designed for use on dogs are available at pet-supply shops. These are the "pliers" type.

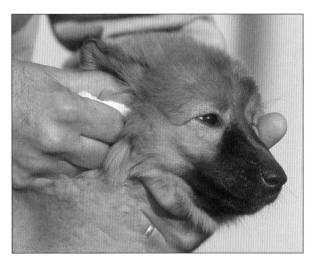

Examine and clean your dog's ears regularly. A soft cotton wipe and ear-cleaning formula should be used for the outer ear. Never probe inside the ear canal.

clipper, and there's no chance of cutting through the quick. Use the grinder on a low setting and always talk soothingly to your dog. He won't mind his salon visit, and he'll have nicely polished nails as well.

Ear Cleaning

Keeping your Tervuren's upright ears clean will protect him from ear infection and ear-mite infestation. In addition, a dog's ears are vulnerable to waxy build-up and to collecting foreign matter from the outdoors. Look in your dog's ears regularly to ensure that they look pink, clean and otherwise healthy. Even if they look fine, an odor in the ears signals a problem and means it's time to call the vet.

Since the Tervuren has upright ears, he is not nearly as apt to have ear problems as might a dog with drop ears. For healthy ears, monthly ear cleaning is recommended; you can do this along with one of your grooming sessions. Using a cotton ball or pad, and never probing into the ear canal, wipe the ear gently. You can use an ear-cleansing liquid or powder available from your vet or pet-supply store; alternatively, you might prefer to use home-made solutions with ingredients like one part white vinegar and one part hydrogen peroxide. Ask your vet about home remedies before you attempt to concoct something on your own.

blood with a styptic pencil or other clotting agent. If you mistakenly nip the quick, do not panic or fuss, as this will cause the pup to be afraid. Simply reassure the pup, stop the bleeding and move on to the next nail.

You may or may not be able to see the quick, so it's best to just clip off a small bit at a time. If you see a dark dot in the center of the nail, this is the quick and your cue to stop clipping. Tell the puppy he's a "good boy" and offer a piece of treat with each nail. You can also use nail-clipping time to examine the footpads, making sure that they are not dry and cracked and that nothing has become embedded in them.

The nail grinder is many owners' first choice. Accustoming the puppy to the sound of the grinder and sensation of the buzz presents fewer challenges than the

Keep your dog's ears free of excess hair by plucking it as needed. If done gently, this will be painless for the dog. Look for wax, brown droppings (a sign of ear mites), redness or any other abnormalities. At the first sign of a problem, contact your veterinarian so that he can prescribe an appropriate medication.

EYE CARE
During grooming sessions, pay extra attention to the condition of your dog's eyes. If the area around the eyes is soiled or if tear-staining has occurred, there are various cleaning agents made especially for this purpose. Look at the dog's eyes to make sure no debris has entered; dogs with large eyes and those who spend time outdoors are especially prone to this.

The signs of an eye infection are obvious: mucus, redness, puffiness, scabs or other signs of irritation. If your dog's eyes become infected, the vet will likely prescribe an antibiotic ointment for treatment. If you notice signs of more serious problems, such as opacities in the eyes, which usually indicate cataracts, consult the vet at once. Taking time to pay attention to your dog's eyes will alert you in the early stages of any problem so that you can get your dog treatment as soon as possible. You could save your dog's sight.

DENTAL CARE
Another essential part of grooming is brushing your dog's teeth and checking his overall oral condition. Studies show that around 80% of dogs experience dental problems by two years of age, and the percentage is higher in older dogs. Therefore, it is highly likely that your dog will have trouble with his teeth and gums unless you are proactive with home dental care.

The most common dental problem in dogs is plaque build-up. If not treated, this causes gum disease, infection and resultant tooth loss. Bacteria from these infections spread throughout the body, affecting the vital organs. Do you need much more convincing to start brushing your dog's teeth? If so, take a good whiff of your dog's breath and read on.

Fortunately, home dental care is rather easy and convenient for pet owners. Specially formulated canine toothpaste is easy to find.

Proper dental care is an essential facet of proper healthcare for your Tervuren. Many serious problems can stem from a lack of dental health.

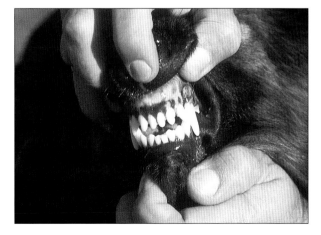

You should use one of these toothpastes, not a product for humans. Some doggie pastes are even available in flavors appealing to dogs. If your dog likes the flavor, he will tolerate the process better, making things much easier for you! Doggie toothbrushes come in different sizes and are designed to fit the contour of a canine mouth. Rubber fingertip brushes fit right on one of your fingers and have rubber nodes to clean the teeth and massage the gums. This may be easier to handle, as it is akin to rubbing your dog's teeth with your finger.

As with other grooming tasks, accustom your pup to his dental care early on. Start gently, for a few minutes at a time, so that he gets used to the feel of the brush and to your handling his mouth. Offer praise and petting so that he looks at tooth-care time as a time when he gets extra love and attention. The routine should become second nature; he may not like it, but he should at least tolerate it.

Aside from brushing, offer dental toys to your dog and feed crunchy biscuits, which help to minimize plaque. Rope toys have the added benefit of acting like floss as the dog chews. At your adult dog's yearly check-ups, the vet will likely perform a thorough tooth scraping as well as a complete check for any problems. Proper care of your dog's teeth will ensure that you will enjoy your dog's smile for many years to come. The next time your dog goes to give you a hello kiss, you'll be glad you spent the time caring for his teeth.

IDENTIFICATION AND TRAVEL

ID FOR YOUR DOG

You love your Belgian Tervuren and want to keep him safe. Of course you take every precaution to prevent his escaping from the yard or becoming lost or stolen. You have a sturdy high fence and you always keep your dog on lead when out and about in public places. If your dog is not properly identified, however, you are overlooking a major aspect of his safety. We hope to never be in a situation where our dog is missing, but we should practice prevention in the unfortunate case

---

PET OR STRAY?

Besides the obvious benefit of providing your contact information to whoever finds your lost dog, an ID tag makes your dog more approachable and more likely to be recovered. A strange dog wandering the neighborhood without a collar and tags will look like a stray, while the collar and tags indicate that the dog is someone's pet. Even if the ID tags become detached from the collar, the collar alone will make a person more likely to pick up the dog.

that this happens; identification greatly increases the chances of your dog's being returned to you.

There are several ways to identify your dog. First, the traditional dog tag should be a staple in your dog's wardrobe, attached to his everyday collar. Tags can be made of sturdy plastic and various metals and should include your contact information so that a person who finds the dog can get in touch with you right away to arrange his return. Many people today enjoy the wide range of decorative tags available, so have fun and create a tag to match your dog's personality. Of course, it is important that the tag stays on the collar, so have a secure "O" ring attachment; you also can explore the type of tag that slides right onto the collar.

In addition to the ID tag, which every dog should wear even if identified by another method, two other forms of identification have become popular: microchipping and tattooing. In microchipping, a tiny scannable chip is painlessly inserted under the dog's skin. The number is registered to you so that, if your lost dog turns up at a clinic or shelter, the chip can be scanned to retrieve your contact information.

The advantage of the microchip is that it is a permanent form of ID, but there are some factors to consider. Several different companies make

microchips, and not all are compatible with the others' scanning devices. It's best to find a company with a universal microchip that can be read by scanners made by other companies as well. It won't do any good to have the dog chipped if the information cannot be retrieved. Also, not every humane society, shelter and clinic is equipped with a scanner, although more and more facilities are equipping themselves. In fact, many shelters microchip dogs that they adopt out to new homes.

Because the microchip is not visible to the eye, the dog must wear a tag that states that he is microchipped so that whoever picks him up will know to have him scanned. He of course also should have a tag with your contact information in case his chip cannot be read. Humane

You should look into boarding facilities before you have to use one so that you find one with which you will be comfortable about leaving your Tervuren.

Never drive with your Tervuren unrestrained in the car. Crates, harnesses and partitions for the back of the vehicle are three options available for your dog.

To ensure that the tattoo is effective in aiding your dog's return to you, the tattoo number must be registered with a national organization. That way, when someone finds a tattooed dog, a phone call to the registry will quickly match the dog with his owner.

HIT THE ROAD

Car travel with your Belgian Tervuren may be limited to necessity only, such as trips to the vet, or you may bring your dog along almost everywhere you go. This will depend much on your individual dog and how he reacts to rides in the car. You can begin desensitizing your dog to car travel as a pup so that it's something that he's used to. Still, some dogs suffer from motion sickness. Your vet may prescribe a medication for this if trips in the car pose a problem for your dog. At the very least, you will need to get him to the vet, so he will need to tolerate these trips with the least amount of hassle possible.

societies and veterinary clinics offer microchipping service, which is usually very affordable.

Though less popular than microchipping, tattooing is another permanent method of ID for dogs. Most vets perform this service, and there are also clinics that perform dog tattooing. This is also an affordable procedure and one that will not cause much discomfort for the dog. It is best to put the tattoo in a visible area, such as the ear, to deter theft. It is sad to say that there are cases of dogs' being stolen and sold to research laboratories, but such laboratories will not accept tattooed dogs.

Start taking your pup on short trips, maybe just around the block to start. If he is fine with short trips, lengthen your rides a little at a time. Start to take him on your errands or just for drives around town. By this time it will be easy to tell whether your dog is a born traveler or would prefer staying at home when you are on the road.

Of course, safety is a concern regarding your Tervuren in the car. First, he must travel securely, not left loose to roam about the car where he could be injured or distract the driver. A young pup can be held by a passenger initially but should soon graduate to a travel crate, which can be the same crate he uses in the home. Other options include a car harness (like a seat belt for dogs) and partitioning the back of the car with a gate made for this purpose.

Bring along what you will need for the dog. He should wear his collar and ID tags, of course, and you should bring his leash, water (and food if a long trip) and clean-up materials for potty breaks and in case of motion sickness. Always keep your dog on his leash when you make stops, and *never* leave him alone in the car. Many a dog has died from the heat inside a closed car; this does not take much time at all. A dog left alone inside a car can also be a target for thieves.

BOARDING

Today there are many options for dog owners who need someone to care for their dogs in certain circumstances. While many think of boarding their dogs as something to do when away on vacation, many others use the services of doggie "daycare" facili-ties, dropping their dogs off to spend the day while they are at work. Many of these facilities offer both long-term and daily care. Many go beyond just boarding and cater to all sorts of needs, with on-site grooming, veterinary care, training classes and even "web-cams" where owners can log onto the Internet and check out what their dogs are up to. Most dogs enjoy the activity and time spent with other dogs.

Before you need to use such a service, check out the ones in your area. Make visits to see the facilities, meet the staff, discuss fees and available services and see whether this is a place where you think your dog will be happy. It is best to do your research in advance so that you're not stuck at the last minute, forced into making a rushed decision without knowing whether the kennel that you've chosen meets your standards. You also can check with your vet's office to see whether they offer boarding for their clients or can recommend a good kennel in the area.

The kennel will need to see proof of your dog's health records and vaccinations so as not to spread illness from dog to dog. Your dog also will need proper identification. Owners usually experience some separation anxiety the first time they have to leave their dog in someone else's care, so it's reassuring to know that the kennel you choose is run by experi-enced, caring, true dog people.

TRAINING YOUR

BELGIAN TERVUREN

BEGINNING WITH A PUPPY OR ADULT

There's a big difference between training an adult dog and training a young puppy. With a young puppy, everything is new. At eight to ten weeks of age, he will be

The rewards of a healthy, well-trained Tervuren are well worth the effort.

experiencing many things, and he has nothing with which to compare these experiences. Up to this point, he has been with his dam and littermates, not one-on-one with people except in his interactions with his breeder and visitors to the litter.

When you first bring the puppy home, he is eager to please you. This means that he accepts doing things your way. During the next couple of months, he will absorb the basis of everything he needs to know for the rest of his life. This early age is even referred to as the "sponge" stage. After that, for the next 18 months, it's up to you to reinforce good manners by building on the foundation that you've established. Once your puppy is reliable in basic commands and behavior and has reached the appropriate age, you may gradually introduce him to some of the interesting sports, games and activities available to pet owners and their dogs.

Raising your puppy is a family affair. Each member of the family must know what rules to set forth for the puppy and how to use the same one-word commands to mean exactly the same thing every time. Even if yours is a large family, one person will soon be considered by the pup to be the leader, the alpha person in his pack, the "boss" who must be obeyed. Often that highly regarded person turns out to be the one who feeds the puppy. Food ranks very high on the puppy's list of important things! That's why your puppy is rewarded with small treats along with verbal praise when he responds to you correctly. As the puppy learns to do what you want him to do, the food rewards are gradually eliminated and only the praise remains. If you

THE RIGHT START

The best advice for a potential dog owner is to start with the very best puppy that money can buy. Don't shop around for a bargain in the newspaper. You're buying a companion, not a used car or a secondhand appliance. The purchase price of the dog represents a very significant part of the investment, but this is indeed a very small sum compared to the expenses of maintaining the dog in good health. If you purchase a well-bred, healthy and sound puppy, you will be starting right. An unhealthy puppy can cost you thousands of dollars in unnecessary veterinary expenses and, possibly, a fortune in heartbreak as well.

were to keep up with the food treats, you could have two problems on your hands—an obese dog and a beggar.

Training begins the minute your Belgian Tervuren puppy steps through the doorway of your home, so don't make the mistake of putting the puppy on the floor and telling him by your actions to "Go for it! Run wild!" Even if this is your first puppy, you must act as if you know what you're doing: be the boss. An uncertain pup may be terrified to move, while a bold one will be ready to take you at your word and start plotting to destroy the house! Before you collected your puppy, you decided where his own special place would be, and

Training your dog can be a family affair, but it is of utmost importance that the training rules for the dog are consistently reinforced by all members of the family.

he has to unlearn many of his previously self-taught habits and general view of the world.

Working with a professional trainer will speed up your progress with an adopted adult dog. You'll need patience, too. Some new rules may be close to impossible for the dog to accept. After all, he's been successful so far by doing everything his way. He may agree with your instruction for a few days and then slip back into his old ways, so you must be just as consistent and understanding in your teaching as you would be with a puppy. Your dog has to learn to pay attention to your voice, your family, the daily routine, new smells, new sounds and, in some cases, even a new climate.

One of the most important things to find out about a newly adopted adult dog is his reaction to children (yours and others), strangers and your friends and how he acts upon meeting other dogs. If he was not socialized with dogs as a puppy, this could be a major problem. This does not mean that he's a "bad" dog, a vicious dog or an aggressive dog; rather, it means that he has no idea how to read another dog's body language. There's no way for him to tell whether the other dog is a friend or foe. Survival instinct takes over, telling him to attack first and ask questions later. This definitely calls for professional help and, even then, may not be a

Before you can teach your dog any lesson, you have to have his undivided attention.

that's where to put him when you first arrive home. Give him a house tour after he has investigated his area, had a nap and gone for a bathroom "pit stop."

It's worth mentioning here that if you've adopted an adult dog that is completely trained to your liking, you are fortunate indeed. However, if that dog spent his life up to this point in a kennel, or even in a good home but without any real training, be prepared to tackle the job ahead. A dog three years of age or older with no previous training cannot be blamed for not knowing what he was never taught. While the dog is trying to understand and learn your rules, at the same time behavior that can be corrected 100% reliably (or even at all). If you have a puppy, this is why it is so very important to introduce your young puppy properly to other puppies and "dog-friendly" adult dogs.

HOUSE-TRAINING YOUR BELGIAN TERVUREN

Dogs are "touch-sensitive" when it comes to house-training. In other words, they respond to the surface on which they are given approval to eliminate. The choice of which surface to offer the dog is yours. The best choice, if you can manage it, is a small area of crushed stone in a corner of the yard. The most common choice, of course, is the lawn, and dogs love everything about grass.

You can start out with paper-training indoors and switch over to an outdoor surface as the puppy matures and gains control over his need to eliminate. Of course, the Belgian Tervuren is too large to paper-train for life, but it is a viable option for puppy training. For the naysayers, don't worry—this won't mean that the dog will soil on every piece of newspaper lying around the house. You are training him to go outside, remember?

PUPPY'S RELIEF TIME

Your puppy's need to relieve himself is seemingly non-stop, but signs of improvement will be

Taking the dog out for potty breaks is everyone's responsibility, not just the adults of the household.

Training includes teaching and enforcing the house rules; for example, will the pup be allowed on the furniture?

seen each week. From 8 to 10 weeks old, the puppy will have to be taken outside every time he wakes up, about 10–15 minutes after every meal and after every period of play—all day long, from first thing in the morning until his bedtime. That's a total of ten or more trips per day to teach the puppy where it's okay to relieve himself. With that schedule in mind, you can see that house-training a young puppy is not a part-time job. It requires someone to be home all day.

If that seems overwhelming, do a little planning. For example, plan to pick up your puppy at the start of a vacation period. If you can't get home in the middle of the day, plan to hire a dog-sitter or ask a neighbor to come over to take the pup outside, feed him his lunch and then take him out again about ten or so minutes after he's eaten. Also make arrangements with that or another person to be your "emergency" contact if you have to stay late on the job. Remind yourself—repeatedly— that this hectic schedule improves as the puppy gets older.

THE PUPPY'S PLACE IN THE HOME
Your Belgian Tervuren puppy needs to be confined to one secure puppy-proof area when no one is able to watch his every move. Generally the kitchen is the place of choice because the floor is washable. Likewise, it's a busy family area that will

---

BASIC PRINCIPLES OF DOG TRAINING

1. Start training early. A young puppy is ready, willing and able.
2. Timing is your all-important tool. Praise at the exact time that the dog responds correctly. Pay close attention.
3. Patience is almost as important as timing!
4. Repeat! The same word has to mean the same thing every time.
5. In the beginning, praise all correct behavior verbally, along with treats and petting.

CANINE DEVELOPMENT SCHEDULE

It is important to understand how and at what age a puppy develops into adulthood.
If you are a puppy owner, consult this Canine Development Schedule to
determine the stage of development your puppy is currently experiencing.
This knowledge will help you as you work with the puppy in the weeks and months ahead.

PERIOD	AGE	CHARACTERISTICS
FIRST TO THIRD	BIRTH TO SEVEN WEEKS	Puppy needs food, sleep and warmth and responds to simple and gentle touching. Needs mother for security and disciplining. Needs littermates for learning and interacting with other dogs. Pup learns to function within a pack and learns pack order of dominance. Begin socializing pup with adults and children for short periods. Pup begins to become aware of his environment.
FOURTH	EIGHT TO TWELVE WEEKS	Brain is fully developed. Pup needs socializing with outside world. Remove from mother and littermates. Needs to change from canine pack to human pack. Human dominance necessary. Fear period occurs between 8 and 12 weeks. Avoid fright and pain.
FIFTH	THIRTEEN TO SIXTEEN WEEKS	Training and formal obedience should begin. Less association with other dogs, more with people, places, situations. Period will pass easily if you remember this is pup's change-to-adolescence time. Be firm and fair. Flight instinct prominent. Permissiveness and over-disciplining can do permanent damage. Praise for good behavior.
JUVENILE	FOUR TO EIGHT MONTHS	Another fear period about seven to eight months of age. It passes quickly, but be cautious of fright and pain. Sexual maturity reached. Dominant traits established. Dog should understand sit, down, come and stay by now.

NOTE: THESE ARE APPROXIMATE TIME FRAMES. ALLOW FOR INDIVIDUAL DIFFERENCES IN PUPPIES.

accustom the pup to a variety of noises, everything from pots and pans to the telephone, blender and dishwasher. He will also be enchanted by the smell of your cooking (and will never be critical when you burn something). An exercise pen (also called an "ex-pen," a puppy version of a playpen) within the room of choice is an excellent means of confinement for a young pup. He can see out and has a certain amount of space in which to run about, but he is safe from dangerous things like electrical cords, heating units, trash baskets or open kitchen-supply cabinets. Place the pen where the puppy will not get a blast of heat or air conditioning.

You select the area in which your Tervuren is to relieve himself. Once trained, he will always return to the same spot.

In the pen, you can put a few toys, his bed (which can be his crate if the dimensions of pen and crate are compatible) and a few layers of newspaper in one small corner, just in case. A water bowl can be hung at a convenient height on the side of the ex-pen so it won't become a splashing pool for an innovative puppy. His food dish can go on the floor, next to but not under the water bowl.

Crates are something that pet owners are at last getting used to for their dogs. Wild or domestic canines have always preferred to sleep in den-like safe spots, and that is exactly what the crate provides. How often have you seen adult dogs that choose to sleep under a table or chair even though they have full run of the house? It's the den connection.

In your "happy" voice, use the word "Crate" every time you put the pup into his den. If he's new to a crate, toss in a small biscuit for him to chase the first few times. At night, after he's been outside, he should sleep in his crate. The crate may be kept in the pup's designated area at night or, if you want to be sure to hear those wake-up yips in the morning, put the crate in a corner of your bedroom. However, don't make any response whatsoever to whining or crying. If he's completely ignored, he'll settle down and get to sleep.

Good bedding for a young puppy is an old folded bath towel or an old blanket, something that is easily washable and disposable if necessary ("accidents" will happen!). Never put newspaper in the puppy's crate. An extremely good breeder would have introduced your puppy to the crate by letting two pups sleep together for a couple of nights, followed by several nights alone. How thankful you will be if you find that breeder!

Safe toys in the pup's crate or area will keep him occupied, but monitor their condition closely. Discard any toys that show signs of being chewed to bits. Squeaky parts, bits of stuffing or plastic or any other small pieces can cause intestinal blockage or possibly choking if ingested.

POTTY-TRAINING PROGRESS

After you've taken your puppy out and he has relieved himself in the area you've selected, he can have some free time with the family as long as there is someone responsible for watching him. That doesn't mean just someone in the same room who is watching TV or busy on the computer, but one person who is doing nothing other than keeping an eye on the pup, playing with him on the floor and helping him understand his position in the pack.

This first taste of freedom will let you begin to set the house rules. If you don't want the dog on the furniture, now is the time to prevent his first attempts to jump up onto the couch. The word to use in this case is "Off," not "Down." "Down" is the word you will use to teach the down position, which is something entirely different.

Most corrections at this stage come in the form of simply distracting the puppy. Instead of telling him "No" for "Don't chew the carpet," distract the chomping puppy with a toy and he'll forget about the carpet.

As you are playing with the pup, do not forget to watch him closely and pay attention to his body language. Whenever you see him begin to circle or sniff, take the puppy outside to relieve himself. If you are paper-training,

Very young puppies need to relieve themselves often and have little control. Their control, of course, improves with age and training.

Scent attraction is what will lead your Tervuren to the same relief spot every time, once you've trained him on where that should be.

and droppings. Regular household cleansers won't do the trick. Pet shops sell the best pet deodorizers. Invest in the largest container you can find.

Scent attraction eventually will lead your pup to his chosen spot outdoors; this is the basis of outdoor training. When you take your puppy outside to relieve himself, use a one-word command such as "Outside" or "Go-potty"

put him back into his confined area on the newspapers. In either case, praise him as he eliminates while he actually is *in the act* of relieving himself. Three seconds after he has finished is too late! You'll be praising him for running toward you, picking up a toy or whatever he may be doing at that moment, and that's not what you want to be praising him for. Timing is a vital tool in all dog training.

If using newspapers, remove soiled newspapers immediately and replace them with clean ones. You may want to take a small piece of soiled paper and place it in the middle of the new clean papers, as the scent will attract him to that spot when it's time to go again. That scent attraction is why it's so important to clean up any messes made in the house by using a product specially made to eliminate the odor of dog urine

SOMEBODY TO BLAME

House-training a puppy can be frustrating for the puppy and the owner alike. The puppy does not instinctively understand the difference between defecating on the pavement outside and on the ceramic tile in the kitchen. He is confused and frightened by his human's exuberant reactions to his natural urges. The owner, arguably the more intelligent of the duo, is also frustrated that he cannot convince his puppy to obey his commands and instructions.

In frustration, the owner may struggle with the temptation to discipline the puppy, scold him or even strike him on the rear end. Harsh corrections are unnecessary and inappropriate, serving to defeat your purpose in gaining your puppy's trust and respect. Don't blame your nine-week-old puppy. Blame yourself for not being 100% consistent in the puppy's lessons and routine. The lesson here is simple: try harder and your puppy will succeed.

(that's one word to the puppy) as you attach his leash. Then lead him to his area. Now comes the hard part—hard for you, that is. Just stand there until he urinates and defecates. Move him a few feet in one direction or another if he's just sitting there looking at you, but remember that this is neither playtime nor time for a walk. This is strictly a business trip. Then, as he circles and squats (remember your timing), give him a quiet "Good dog" as praise. If you start to jump for joy, ecstatic over his performance, he'll do one of two things: either he will stop mid-stream, as it were, or he'll do it again for you— in the house—and expect you to be just as delighted.

Give him five minutes or so and, if he doesn't go in that time, take him back indoors to his confined area and try again in another ten minutes, or immediately if you see him sniffing and circling. By careful observation, you'll soon work out a successful schedule.

Accidents, by the way, are just that—accidents. Clean them up quickly and thoroughly, without comment, after the puppy has been taken outside to finish his business and then put back into his area or crate. If you witness an accident in progress, say "No!" in a stern voice and get the pup outdoors immediately. No punishment is needed. You

and your puppy are just learning each other's language, and sometimes it's easy to miss a puppy's message. Chalk it up to experience and watch more closely from now on.

AN ORDERLY PACK

Discipline is a form of training that brings order to life. For example, military discipline is what allows the soldiers in an army to work as one. Discipline is a form of teaching and, in dogs, is the basis of how the successful pack operates. Each member knows his place in the pack and all respect the leader or alpha dog. It is essential for your puppy that you establish

A dog who trusts his master completely won't be averse to a belly rub now and then. This posture is the most submissive of all canine body language.

this type of relationship, with you as the alpha, or leader. It is a form of social coexistence that all canines recognize and accept. Discipline, therefore, is never to be confused with punishment. When you teach your puppy how you want him to behave, and he behaves properly and you praise him for it, you are disciplining him with a form of positive reinforcement.

Before you can start any type of training, your puppy must be used to and comfortable with his collar.

WHO'S TRAINING WHOM?

Dog training is a black-and-white exercise. The correct response to a command must be absolute, and the trainer must insist on completely accurate responses from the dog. A trainer cannot command his dog to sit and then settle for the dog's melting into the down position. Often owners are so pleased that their dogs "did something" in response to a command that they just shrug and say, "OK, Down" even though they wanted the dog to sit. You want your dog to respond to the command without hesitation. He must respond at that moment and correctly every time.

For a dog, rewards come in the form of praise, a smile, a cheerful tone of voice, a few friendly pats or a rub of the ears. Rewards are also small food treats. Obviously, that does not mean bits of regular dog food. Instead, treats are very small bits of special things like cheese or pieces of soft dog treats. The idea is to reward the dog with something very small that he can taste and swallow, providing instant positive reinforcement. If he has to take time to chew the treat, he will have forgotten what he did to earn it by the time he is finished.

Your puppy should never be physically punished. The displeasure shown on your face and in your voice is sufficient to signal to the pup that he has done something wrong. He wants to please everyone higher up on the social ladder, especially his leader, so a scowl and harsh voice will take care of the error. Growling out the word "Shame!" when the pup is caught in the act of doing something wrong is better than the repetitive "No." Some dogs hear "No" so often that they begin to think it's their name! By the way, do not use the dog's name when you're correcting him. His name is reserved to get his attention for something pleasant about to take place.

There are punishments that have nothing to do with you. For example, your dog may think that chasing cats is one reason for his existence. You can try to stop it as much as you like but without success, because it's such fun for

KIDS RULE
Children of 10 to 12 year of age are old enough to understand the "be kind to dumb animals" approach and will have fun training their dogs, especially to do tricks. It teaches them to be tolerant, patient and appreciative as well as to accept failure to some extent. Young children can be tyrants, making unreasonable demands of the dog and unable to cope with defeat, blaming it all on the dog. Toddlers need not apply for the job of dog trainer.

the dog. But one good hissing, spitting swipe of a cat's claws across the dog's nose will put an end to the game forever. Intervene only when your dog's eyeball is seriously at risk. Cat scratches can cause permanent damage to an innocent but annoying puppy.

PUPPY KINDERGARTEN

COLLAR AND LEASH
Before you begin your Tervuren puppy's education, he must be used to his collar and leash. Choose a collar for your puppy that is secure, but not heavy or bulky. He won't enjoy training if

Your puppy must also be accustomed to his leash before you can teach commands. All members of the family can help by spending time gently leading the pup around the house or yard.

The key to all training is keeping your Tervuren's attention; a distraction-free training area is a must.

at the end of the leash. The leash used to take the puppy outside to relieve himself is shorter because you don't want him to roam away from his area. The shorter leash will also be the one to use when you walk the puppy.

If you've been wise enough to enroll in a puppy kindergarten training class, suggestions will be made as to the best collar and leash for your young puppy. I say "wise" because your puppy will be in a class with puppies in his age range (up to five months old) of all breeds and sizes. It's the perfect

he's uncomfortable. A flat buckle collar is fine for everyday wear and for initial puppy training. For older dogs, there are several types of training collars such as the martingale, which is a double loop that tightens slightly around the neck, or the head collar, which is similar to a horse's halter. Do not use a chain choke collar unless you have been specifically shown how to put it on and how to use it. You may not be disposed to use a chain choke collar even if your breeder has told you that it's suitable for your Belgian Tervuren.

A lightweight 6-foot woven cotton or nylon training leash is preferred by most trainers because it is easy to fold up in your hand and comfortable to hold because there is a certain amount of give to it. There are lessons where the dog will start off 6 feet away from you

LEASH TRAINING

House-training and leash training go hand in hand, literally. When taking your puppy outside to do his business, lead him there on his leash. Unless an emergency potty run is called for, do not whisk the puppy up into your arms and take him outside. If you have a fenced yard, you have the advantage of letting the puppy loose to go out, but it's better to put the dog on the leash and take him to his designated place in the yard until he is reliably house-trained. Taking the puppy for a walk is the best way to house-train a dog. The dog will associate the walk with his time to relieve himself, and the exercise of walking stimulates the dog's bowels and bladder. Dogs that are not trained to relieve themselves on a walk may hold it until they get back home, which of course defeats half the purpose of the walk.

SIT AROUND THE HOUSE

"Sit" is the command you'll use most often. Your pup will likely object when placed in a sit with your hands, so try the "bringing the food up under his chin" method. Better still, catch him in the act! Your dog will sit on his own many times throughout the day, so let him know that he's doing the "Sit" by rewarding him. Praise him and have him sit for everything—toys, connecting his leash, his dinner, before going out the door, etc.

way for him to learn the right way (and the wrong way) to interact with other dogs as well as their people. You cannot teach your puppy how to interpret another dog's sign language. For a first-time puppy owner, these socialization classes are invaluable. For experienced dog owners, they are a real boon to further training.

ATTENTION

You've been using the dog's name since the minute you collected him from the breeder, so you should be able to get his attention by saying his name—with a big smile and in an excited tone of voice. His response will be the puppy equivalent of "Here I am! What are we going to do?" Your immediate response is "Good dog." Rewarding him at the moment he pays attention to you teaches him the proper way to

respond when he hears his name. To keep the pup's attention for training, choose a distraction-free area. For his safety, begin all lessons on lead and only progress to off-leash training in enclosed areas and once the exercise has been learned reliably on lead.

COMMAND CENTRAL FOR THE EDUCATED TERVUREN

THE SIT COMMAND

There are several ways to teach the puppy to sit. The first one is to catch him whenever he is about

You will have a much easier time training your adult Terv if he looks up to you as his trusted leader.

In teaching the sit, you may have to begin by guiding your dog into the sit position until he gets the idea.

point, he will have to either sit or fall over, so as his back legs buckle under, say "Sit, good dog," and then give him the treat and lots of praise. You may have to begin with your hand lightly running up his chest, actually lifting his chin up until he sits. Some (usually older) dogs require gentle pressure on their hindquarters with the left hand, in which case the dog should be on your left side. Puppies generally do not appreciate this physical dominance.

After a few times, you should be able to show the dog a treat in the open palm of your hand, raise your hand waist-high as you say "Sit" and have him sit. You thereby will have taught him two things at the same time. Both the verbal command and the motion of the hand are signals for the sit. Your puppy is watching you almost more than

to sit and, as his backside nears the floor, say "Sit, good dog!" That's positive reinforcement and, if your timing is sharp, he will learn that what he's doing at that second is connected to your saying "Sit" and that you think he's clever for doing it.

Another method is to start with the puppy on his leash in front of you. Show him a treat in the palm of your right hand. Bring your hand up under his nose and, almost in slow motion, move your hand up and back so his nose goes up in the air and his head tilts back as he follows the treat in your hand. At that

OKAY!
This is the signal that tells your dog that he can quit whatever he was doing. Use "Okay" to end a session on a correct response to a command. (Never end on an incorrect response.) Lots of praise follows. People use "Okay" a lot and it has other uses for dogs, too. Your dog is barking. You say, "Okay! Come!" "Okay" signals him to stop the barking activity and "Come" allows him to come to you for a "Good dog."

he is listening to you, so what you do is just as important as what you say.

Don't save any of these drills only for training sessions. Use them as much as possible at odd times during a normal day. The dog should always sit before being given his food dish. He should sit to let you go through a doorway first, when the doorbell rings or when you stop to speak to someone on the street.

THE DOWN COMMAND

Before beginning to teach the down exercise, you must consider how the dog feels about this exercise. To him, "down" is a submissive position. Being flat on the floor with you standing over him is not his idea of fun. It's up to you to let him know that, while it may not be fun, the reward of your approval is worth his effort.

Start with the puppy on your left side in a sit position. Hold the leash right above his collar in your left hand. Have an extra-special treat, such as a small piece of cooked chicken or hot dog, in your right hand. Place it at the end of the pup's nose and steadily move your hand down and forward along the ground. Hold the leash to prevent a sudden lunge for the food. As the puppy goes into the down position, say "Down" very gently.

The difficulty with this exercise is twofold: it's both the

As the dog becomes comfortable in the down position, he will respond to your verbal command with no physical guidance or treat.

submissive aspect and the fact that most people say the word "Down" as if they were drill sergeants in charge of recruits! So issue the command sweetly, give him the treat and have the pup maintain the down position for several seconds. If he tries to get up immediately, place your hands on his shoulders and press down gently, giving him a very quiet "Good dog." As you progress with this lesson, increase the "down time" until he will hold it until you say "Okay" (his cue for release).

Practice this one in the house at various times throughout the day.

By increasing the length of time during which the dog must maintain the down position, you'll find many uses for it. For example, he can lie at your feet in the vet's office or anywhere that both of you have to wait, when you are on the phone, while the family is eating and so forth. If you progress to training for competitive obedience, he'll already be all set for the exercise called the long down.

THE STAY COMMAND

You can teach your Belgian Tervuren to stay in the sit, down and stand positions. To teach the sit/stay, have the dog sit on your left side. Hold the leash at waist level in your left hand and let the dog know that you have a treat in your closed right hand. Step forward on your right foot as you say "Stay." Immediately turn and stand directly in front of the dog, keeping your right hand up high so he'll keep his eye on the treat hand and maintain the sit position for a count of five. Return to your original position and offer the reward.

Increase the length of the sit/stay each time until the dog can hold it for at least 30 seconds without moving. After about a week of success, move out on your right foot and take two steps before turning to face the dog. Give the "Stay" hand signal (left palm back toward the dog's head) as you leave. He gets the treat when you return and he holds the sit/stay. Increase the distance that you walk away from him before turning until you reach the length of your training leash. But don't rush it! Go back to the beginning if he moves before he should. No matter what the lesson, never be upset by having to back up for a few days. The repetition and practice are what will make your dog reliable in these commands. It won't do any good to move on to something more difficult if the command is not mastered at the easier levels. Above all, even if you do get frustrated, never let your puppy know! Always keep a positive, upbeat attitude during training, which will transmit to your dog for positive results.

The down/stay is taught in the same way once the dog is completely reliable and steady with the down command. Again, don't rush it. With the dog in the down position on your left side, step out on your right foot as you say "Stay." Return by walking around in back of the dog and into your original position. While you are training, it's okay to murmur something like "Hold on" to encourage him to stay put. When the dog will stay without moving when you are at a distance of 3 or 4 feet, begin to increase the length of time before you return. Be sure he holds the down on your return until you say "Okay." At that point, he gets his treat—just so he'll remember for next time that it's not over until it's over.

THE COME COMMAND

No command is more important to the safety of your Belgian Tervuren than "Come." It is what you should say every single time you see the puppy running toward you: "Piper, come! Good dog." During playtime, run a few feet away from the puppy and turn and tell him to "Come" as he is already running to you. You can go so far as to teach your puppy two things at once if you squat down and hold out your arms. As the pup gets close to you and you're saying "Good dog," bring your right arm in about waist high. Now he's also learning the hand signal, an excellent device should you be on the phone when you need to get

him to come to you! You'll also both be one step ahead when you enter obedience classes.

When the puppy responds to your well-timed "Come," try it with the puppy on the training leash. This time, catch him off guard, while he's sniffing a leaf or

---

COME AND GET IT!

The come command is your dog's safety signal. Until he is 99% perfect in responding, don't use the come command if you cannot enforce it. Practice on leash with treats or squeakers or whenever the dog is running to you. Never call him to come to you if he is to be corrected for a misdemeanor. Reward the dog with a treat and happy praise whenever he comes to you.

With a dog as athletic and strong as the Tervuren, teaching your Belgian to behave on lead is essential.

Never call the dog to come to you—with or without his name—if you are angry or intend to correct him for some misbehavior. When correcting the pup, you go to him. Your dog must always connect "Come" with something pleasant and with your approval; then you can rely on his response.

Puppies, like children, have notoriously short attention spans, so don't overdo it with any of the training. Keep each lesson short. Break it up with a quick run around the yard or a ball toss, repeat the lesson and quit as soon as the pup gets it right. That way, you will always end with a "Good dog."

Life isn't perfect and neither are puppies. A time will come, often around ten months of age, when he'll become "selectively deaf" or choose to "forget" his name. He may respond by wagging his tail (and even seeming to smile at you) with a look that says "Make me!" Laugh, throw his favorite toy and skip the lesson you had planned. Pups will be pups!

watching a bird: "Piper, come!" You may have to pause for a split second after his name to be sure you have his attention. If the puppy shows any sign of confusion, give the leash a mild jerk and take a couple of steps backward. Do not repeat the command. In this case, you should say "Good come" as he reaches you.

That's the number-one rule of training. Each command word is given just once. Anything more is nagging. You'll also notice that all commands are one word only. Even when they are actually two words, you say them as one.

THE HEEL COMMAND

The second most important exercise to teach, after the come, is the heel. When you are walking your growing puppy, you need to be in control. Besides, it looks terrible to be pulled and yanked down the street, and it's not much fun either. Your eight- to ten-week-old puppy will probably follow you everywhere, but that's his natural instinct, not your control over the situation. However, any time he does follow you, you can say "Heel" and be ahead of the game, as he will learn to associate this command with the action of following you before you even begin teaching him to heel.

There is a very precise, almost military, procedure for teaching your dog to heel. As with all other obedience training, begin with the dog on your left side. He will be in a very nice sit and you will have the training leash across your chest. Hold the loop and folded leash in your right hand. Pick up the slack leash above the dog in your left hand and hold it loosely at your side. Step out on your left foot as you say "Heel." If

FROM HEEL TO ETERNITY

To begin, step away from the dog, who is in the sit position, on your left foot. That tells the dog you aren't going anywhere. Turn and stand directly in front of him so he won't be tempted to follow. Two seconds is a long, long time to your dog, so increase the time for which he's expected to stay only in short increments. Don't force it. When practicing the heel exercise, your dog will sit at your side whenever you stop. Don't stop for more than three seconds, as your enthusiastic dog will really feel that it's an eternity!

the puppy does not move, give a gentle tug or pat your left leg to get him started. If he surges ahead of you, stop and pull him back gently until he is at your side. Tell him to sit and begin again.

Walk a few steps and stop while the puppy is correctly beside you. Tell him to sit and give mild verbal praise. (More enthusiastic praise will encourage him to think the lesson is over.) Repeat the lesson, increasing the number of steps you take only as long as the dog is heeling nicely beside you. When you end the lesson, have him hold the sit, then

As you progress with your Tervuren's training, you will use treats more sparingly, but never skimp on the praise.

Once you have the basics down pat, you and your Tervuren may want to take his training further by preparing for obedience classes.

Staying and heeling can take a lot out of a dog, so provide playtime and free-running exercise to shake off the stress when the lessons are over. You don't want him to associate training with all work and no fun.

BREAKING THE TREAT HABIT

Your dog has been watching you—and the hand that treats—throughout all of his lessons, and now it's time to break the treat habit. Begin by giving him treats at the end of each lesson only. Then start to give a treat after the end of only some of the lessons. At the end of every lesson, as well as during the lessons, be consistent with the praise. Your pup now doesn't know whether he'll get a treat or not, but he should keep performing well just in case! Finally, you will stop giving treat rewards entirely. Save them for something brand-new that you want to teach him. Keep up the praise and you'll always have a "good dog."

give him the "Okay" to let him know that this is the end of the lesson. Praise him so that he knows he did a good job.

The cure for excessive pulling (a common problem) is to stop when the dog is no more than 2 or 3 feet ahead of you. Guide him back into position and begin again. With a really determined puller, try switching to a head collar. This will automatically turn the pup's head toward you so you can bring him back easily to the heel position. Give quiet, reassuring praise every time the leash goes slack and he's staying with you.

OBEDIENCE CLASSES

The advantages of an obedience class are that your dog will have to learn amid the distractions of other people and dogs and that your mistakes will be quickly corrected by the trainer. Teaching your dog along with a qualified instructor and other handlers who may have more dog experience than you is another plus of the class environ-

> **I WILL FOLLOW YOU**
>
> Obedience isn't just a classroom activity. In your home you have many great opportunities to teach your dog polite manners. Allowing your pet on the bed or furniture elevates him to your level, which is not a good idea (the word is "Off!"). Use the "umbilical cord" method, keeping your dog on lead so he has to go with you wherever you go. You sit, he sits. You walk, he heels. You stop, he sit/stays. Everywhere you go, he's with you, but you go first!

ment. The instructor and other handlers can help you to find the most efficient way of teaching your dog a command or exercise. It's often easier to learn from other people's mistakes than your own. You will also learn all of the requirements for competitive obedience trials, in which you can earn titles and go on to advanced jumping and retrieving exercises, which are fun for many dogs. Obedience classes build the foundation needed for many other canine activities (in which we humans are allowed to participate, too!).

TRAINING FOR OTHER ACTIVITIES

Because the Belgian shepherds are among the most versatile and intelligent of all breeds of dog, you can nearly take your pick of the activities that you would like to participate in with your Tervuren. Your dog will be up to the task and will be an active participant and a quick learner. Of course, advanced training requires an owner who also likes to do high-energy activities and is willing to take the time to train and to work with his dog.

When your puppy has a good grasp of the basic commands, whether taught in a class or at home, you should check out training classes that prepare dogs for obedience competition. Decide which style of training appeals to you, as there are many different philosophies on training dogs. Obedience is a natural for Tervurens and it may be for you, too. Tervurens are very capable of progressing through the levels of obedience competition and achieving difficult-to-attain titles.

Agility, started in England, has become a very popular sport in America and can be easily found at dog shows. Look for the large, noisy ring filled with competitors and dogs running the course and excited spectators watching at ringside and cheering as if at a football game. Dogs are taught to conquer an obstacle course with their handlers running beside them, shouting directions and encouragement. The AKC defines agility as, "The enjoyment of bringing together communication, training, timing, accuracy

Although herding is instinctual in the breed, not every Tervuren is equally as good at the job. Some require more (and different) training.

and just plain fun in the ultimate game for you and your dog." Not to mention that it's plenty of physical and mental exercise for both dog and owner.

Flyball is a team relay race that requires cooperation between handlers and their dogs. Each dog is required to run down a lane, go over jumps, catch a ball at the end of the lane and return to his owner, at which point the second participant in the relay goes through the same course. The team to finish in the best time wins. Again, another sport that is active, fun and noisy!

And, of course, there is herding, which the Belgians are bred to do. It is a Belgian Tervuren's natural instinct to herd animals as well as his humans! The earliest herding

trial on record was held in Wales in 1873, and since that date, herding trials have been held throughout the world for the canines who excel at bringing home (or taking to market) livestock. Herding tests and trials have become a popular sport among Tervuren owners who want to work with and test their dogs' natural abilities.

The Tervuren also has an aptitude for police work and Schutzhund, both of which require intense and demanding training. If you should go into either of these activities, be sure to research training facilities and talk to trainers to determine if this endeavor is for you and your dog. There are some breeders of Belgian Tervurens who breed specifically for the working-type dog. If this is the field you want to get into, you should contact a reputable breeder with experience in police and/or Schutzhund training, who can be found through the American Belgian Tervuren Club.

Search and rescue is another area where the Tervuren's keen intellect will shine. Search and rescue dogs are trained for rescue in water and on all types of terrain and work well in disaster areas, such as after avalanches, hurricanes, building collapses, etc. The owner of a search and rescue dog must be highly motivated as well, as the handler must undergo rigorous training and work right alongside his dog. Belgians can also do very well at tracking, which is often used to locate missing children or adults. Tracking can also be done on a competitive level, with tracking tests held by the AKC and other clubs.

For those who like to volunteer, there is the wonderful feeling of owning a therapy dog and visiting hospices, nursing homes, veterans' homes and childrens' homes and other facilities to bring smiles, comfort and companionship to those who live there. Tervurens excel as therapy dogs.

As you can see, you can take your pick as to which activity will be best for you and your dog. Many owners and their dogs enjoy more than one of these activities but choose to concentrate on only one. However, many Tervurens and their owners excel in more than one field and gain numerous titles to add to the end of their dogs' names.

As wonderful as this list of activities sounds, they all require time and diligence on your part. No dog can learn these activities, and learn them well, without an active, participating owner. However, once you succeed at any of these activities, you and your Tervuren will have a wonderful sense of accomplishment and you will continue to strive for higher and higher levels of achievement.

HOW DO I GET TO CARNEGIE HALL?

Or the National Obedience Championships? The same way you get your dog to do anything else—practice, practice, practice. It's *how* you practice that counts. Keep sessions positive, short, varied, interesting and interspersed with active fun. A bored dog isn't learning. If you're feeling out of sorts yourself, quit for the day. Set yourself a reasonable schedule for several brief practice sessions every day and stick to it. Practice randomly throughout the day as you're doing different things around the house. And give lots of praise for that good "Sit" in front of the TV or while waiting for his dinner!

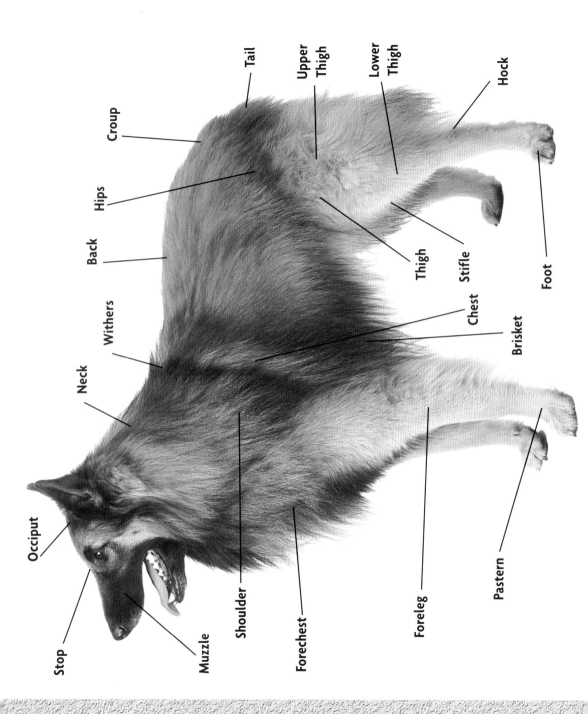

Tail

Upper Thigh

Lower Thigh

Hock

Croup

Hips

Back

Withers

Neck

Occiput

Stop

Muzzle

Shoulder

Forechest

Thigh

Stifle

Foot

Chest

Brisket

Foreleg

Pastern

PHYSICAL STRUCTURE OF THE BELGIAN TERVUREN

BELGIAN TERVUREN

BY LOWELL ACKERMAN, DVM, DACVD

HEALTHCARE FOR A LIFETIME

When you own a dog, you become his healthcare advocate over his entire lifespan, as well as being the one to shoulder the financial burden of such care. Accordingly, it is worthwhile to focus on prevention rather than treatment, as you and your pet will both be happier.

Of course, the best place to have begun your program of preventive healthcare is with the initial purchase or adoption of your dog. There is no way of guaranteeing that your new furry friend is free of medical problems, but there are some things you can do to improve your odds. You certainly should have done adequate research into the Belgian Tervuren and have selected your puppy carefully rather than buying on impulse. Health issues aside, a large number of pet abandonment and relinquishment cases arise from a mismatch between pet needs and owner expectations. This is entirely preventable with appropriate planning and finding a good breeder.

Regarding healthcare issues specifically, it is very difficult to make blanket statements about where to acquire a problem-free pet, but, again, a reputable breeder is your best bet. In an ideal situation you have the opportunity to see both parents, get references from other owners of the breeder's pups and see genetic-testing documentation for several generations of the litter's ancestors. At the very least, you must thoroughly investigate the Belgian Tervuren and the problems inherent in that breed, as well as the genetic testing available to screen for those problems. Genetic testing offers some important benefits, but testing is available for only a few disorders in a relatively small number of breeds and is not available for some of the most common genetic diseases, such as hip dysplasia, cataracts, epilepsy, cardiomyopathy, etc. This area of research is indeed exciting and increasingly important, and advances will continue to be made each year. In fact, recent research has shown that there is

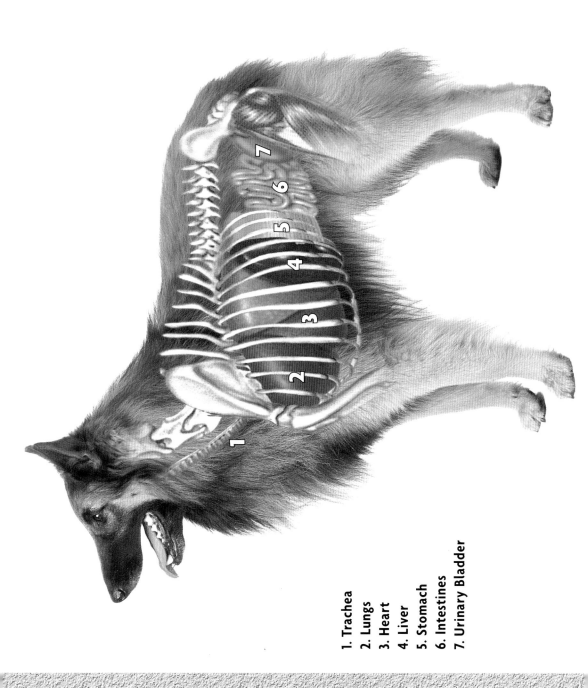

1. Trachea
2. Lungs
3. Heart
4. Liver
5. Stomach
6. Intestines
7. Urinary Bladder

INTERNAL ORGANS OF THE BELGIAN TERVUREN

an equivalent dog gene for 75% of known human genes, so research done in either species is likely to benefit the other.

We've also discussed that evaluating the behavioral nature of your Belgian Tervuren and that of his immediate family members is an important part of the selection process that cannot be overemphasized. It is sometimes difficult to evaluate temperament in puppies because certain behavioral tendencies, such as some forms of aggression, may not be immediately evident. More dogs are euthanized each year for behavioral reasons than for all medical conditions combined, so it is critical to take temperament issues seriously. Start with a well-balanced, friendly companion and put the time and effort into proper socialization, and you will both be rewarded with a lifelong, valued relationship.

Assuming that you have started off with a pup from healthy, sound stock, you then become responsible for helping your veterinarian keep your pet healthy. Some crucial things happen before you even bring your puppy home. Parasite control typically begins at two weeks of age, and vaccinations typically begin at six to eight weeks of age. A pre-pubertal evaluation is typically scheduled for about six months of age. At this time, a dental evaluation is done (since the adult teeth are now in), heartworm prevention is started and neutering or spaying is most commonly done.

It is critical to commence regular dental care at home if you have not already done so. It may not sound very important, but most dogs have active periodontal disease by four years of age if they don't have their teeth cleaned regularly at home, not just at their veterinary exams. Dental problems lead to more than just bad "doggy breath." Gum disease can have very serious medical consequences. If you start brushing your dog's teeth and using antiseptic rinses from a young age, your dog will be accustomed to it and will not resist. The results will be healthy dentition, which your pet will need to enjoy a long, healthy life.

DOGGIE DENTAL CONCERNS

A veterinary dental exam is necessary if you notice one or any combination of the following in your dog:

- Broken, loose or missing teeth
- Loss of appetite (which could be due to mouth pain or illness caused by infection)
- Gum abnormalities, including redness, swelling and bleeding
- Drooling, with or without blood
- Yellowing of the teeth or gumline, indicating tartar
- Bad breath

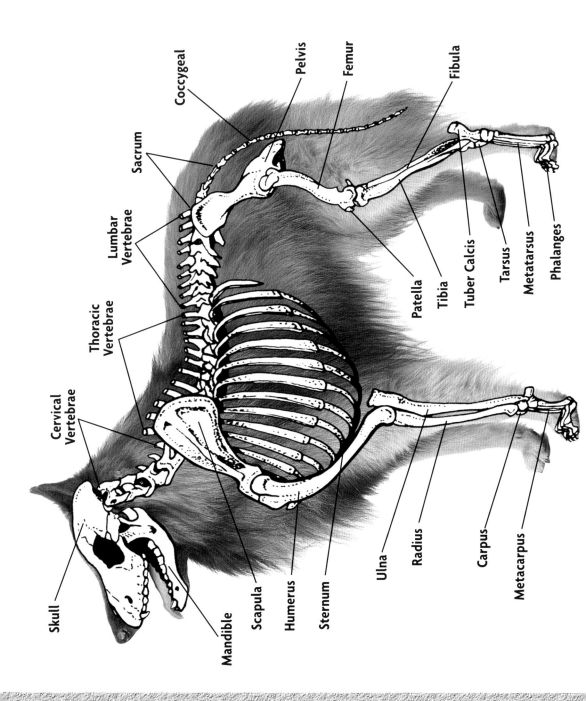

Coccygeal

Pelvis

Femur

Fibula

Sacrum

Lumbar Vertebrae

Thoracic Vertebrae

Cervical Vertebrae

Patella

Tibia

Tuber Calcis

Tarsus

Metatarsus

Phalanges

Skull

Mandible

Scapula

Humerus

Sternum

Ulna

Radius

Carpus

Metacarpus

SKELETAL STRUCTURE OF THE BELGIAN TERVUREN

TAKING YOUR DOG'S TEMPERATURE

It is important to know how to take your dog's temperature at times when you think he may be ill. It's not the most enjoyable task, but it can be done without too much difficulty. It's easier with a helper, preferably someone with whom the dog is friendly, so that one of you can hold the dog while the other inserts the thermometer.

Before inserting the thermometer, coat the end with petroleum jelly. Insert the thermometer slowly and gently into the dog's rectum about one inch. Wait for the reading, about two minutes. Be sure to remove the thermometer carefully and clean it thoroughly after each use.

A dog's normal body temperature is between 100.5 and 102.5 degrees F. Immediate veterinary attention is required if the dog's temperature is below 99 or above 104 degrees F.

Most dogs are considered adults at around a year of age, although some larger breeds still have some filling out to do up to about two or so years old. Even individual dogs within each breed have different healthcare requirements, so work with your veterinarian to determine what will be needed and what your role should be. This doctor-client relationship is important, because as vaccination guidelines change, there may not be an annual "vaccine visit"

scheduled. You must make sure that you see your veterinarian at least annually, even if no vaccines are due, because this is the best opportunity to coordinate health-care activities and to make sure that no medical issues creep by unaddressed.

When your Belgian Tervuren reaches about three-quarters of his anticipated lifespan, he is considered a "senior" and likely requires some special care. In general, if you've been taking great care of your canine companion throughout his formative and adult years, the transition to senior status should be a smooth one. Age is not a disease, and as long as everything is functioning as it should, there is no reason why most of late adulthood should not be rewarding for both you and your pet. This is especially true if you have tended to the details, such as regular veterinary visits, proper dental care, excellent nutrition and management of bone and joint issues.

At this stage in your Belgian Tervuren's life, your veterinarian should start to schedule visits twice yearly, instead of once, to run some laboratory screenings, electrocardiograms and the like, and to change the diet to something more digestible. Catching problems early is the best way to manage them effectively. Treating the early stages of heart disease is so much easier than trying to intervene when there is more significant damage to the heart muscle. Similarly, managing the beginning of kidney problems is fairly routine if there is no significant kidney damage. Other problems, like cognitive dysfunction (similar to senility and Alzheimer's disease), cancer (the Tervuren can be prone to some types), diabetes and arthritis, are more common in older dogs, but all can be treated to help the dog live as many happy, comfortable years as possible. Just as in people, medical management is more effective (and less expensive) when you catch things early.

SELECTING A VETERINARIAN

There is probably no more important decision that you will make regarding your pet's health-care than the selection of his doctor. Your pet's veterinarian will be a pediatrician, family-practice physician and gerontologist, depending on the dog's life stage, and will be the individual who makes recommendations regarding issues such as when specialists need to be consulted, when diagnostic testing and/or therapeutic intervention is needed and when you will need to seek outside emergency and critical-care services. Your vet will act as your advocate and liaison throughout these processes.

Everyone has his own idea about what to look for in a vet, an individual who will play a big role in his dog's (and, of course, his own) life for many years to come. For some, it is the compassionate caregiver with whom they hope to develop a professional relationship to span the lifetime of their dogs and even their future pets. For others, they are seeking a clinician with keen diagnostic and therapeutic insight who can deliver state-of-the-art healthcare. Still others need a veterinary facility that is open evenings and weekends, is in close proximity or provides mobile veterinary services to accommodate their schedules; these people may not much mind that their dogs might see different veterinarians on each visit. Just as we have different reasons for selecting our own healthcare professionals (e.g., covered by insurance plan, expert in field, convenient location, etc.), we should not expect that there is a one-size-fits-all recommendation for selecting a veterinarian and veterinary practice. The best advice is to be honest in your assessment of what you expect from a veterinary practice and to conscientiously research the options in your area. You will quickly appreciate that not all veterinary practices are the same, and you will be happiest with one that truly meets your needs.

There is another point to be considered in the selection of veterinary services. Not that long ago, a single veterinarian would attempt to manage all medical and surgical issues as they arose. That was often problematic, because veterinarians are trained in many species and many diseases, and it was just impossible for general veterinary practitioners to be experts in every species, every breed, every field and every ailment. However, just as in the human healthcare fields, specialization has allowed general practitioners to concentrate on primary healthcare delivery, especially wellness and the prevention of infectious diseases, and to utilize a network of specialists to assist in the management of conditions that require specific expertise and experience. Thus there are now many types of veterinary specialists, including dermatologists, cardiologists, ophthalmologists, surgeons, internists, oncologists, neurologists, behaviorists, critical-ists and others to help primary-care veterinarians deal with complicated medical challenges. In most cases, specialists see cases referred by primary-care veterinarians, make diagnoses and set up management plans. From there, the animals' ongoing care is returned to their primary-care veterinarians. This important team approach to your pet's medical-care needs has provided

DOGGIE INSURANCE
Pet insurance policies are very cost-effective (and very inexpensive by human health-insurance standards), but make sure that you buy the policy long before you intend to use it (preferably starting in puppyhood, because coverage will exclude pre-existing conditions) and that you are actually buying an indemnity insurance plan from an insurance company that is regulated by your state or province. Many insurance policy look-alikes are actually discount clubs that are redeemable only at specific locations and for specific services. An indemnity plan covers your pet at almost all veterinary, specialty and emergency practices and is an excellent way to manage your pet's ongoing healthcare needs.

opportunities for advanced care and an unparalleled level of quality to be delivered.

With all of the opportunities for your Belgian Tervuren to receive high-quality veterinary medical care, there is another topic that needs to be addressed at the same time—cost. It's been said that you can have excellent healthcare or inexpensive healthcare, but never both; this is as true in veterinary medicine as it is in human medicine. While veterinary costs are a fraction of what the same services cost in the human healthcare arena, it is still difficult to deal with unanticipated medical costs, especially since they can easily creep into hundreds or even thousands of dollars if specialists or emergency services become involved. However, there are ways of managing these risks. The easiest is to buy pet health insurance and realize that its foremost purpose is not to cover routine healthcare visits but rather to serve as an umbrella for those rainy days when your pet needs medical care and you don't want to worry about whether or not you can afford that care.

VACCINATIONS AND INFECTIOUS DISEASES

There has never been an easier time to prevent a variety of infectious diseases in your dog, but the advances we've made in veterinary medicine come with a price—choice. Now while it may seem that choice is a good thing (and it is), it has never been more difficult for the pet owner (or the veterinarian) to make an informed decision about the best way to protect pets through vaccination.

Years ago, it was just accepted that puppies got a starter series of vaccinations and then annual "boosters" throughout their lives to keep them protected. As more and more vaccines became available, consumers wanted the convenience of having all of that protection in a single injection. The result was "multivalent"

vaccines that crammed a lot of protection into a single syringe. The manufacturers' recommendations were to give the vaccines annually, and this was a simple enough protocol to follow. However, as veterinary medicine has become more sophisticated and we have started looking more at healthcare quandaries rather than convenience, it became necessary to reevaluate the situation and deal with some tough questions. It is important to realize that whether or not to use a particular vaccine depends on the risk of contracting the disease against which it protects, the severity of the disease if it is contracted, the duration of immunity provided by the vaccine, the safety of the product and the needs of the individual animal. In a very general sense, rabies, distemper, hepatitis and parvovirus are considered core vaccine needs, while parainfluenza, *Bordetella bronchiseptica*, leptospirosis, coronavirus and borreliosis (Lyme disease) are considered non-core needs and best reserved for animals that demonstrate reasonable risk of contracting the diseases.

NEUTERING/SPAYING

Sterilization procedures (neutering for males/spaying for females) are meant to accomplish several purposes. While the underlying premise is to address

COMMON INFECTIOUS DISEASES

Let's discuss some of the diseases that create the need for vaccination in the first place. Following are the major canine infectious diseases and a simple explanation of each.

Rabies: A devastating viral disease that can be fatal in dogs and people. In fact, vaccination of dogs and cats is an important public-health measure to create a resistant animal buffer population to protect people from contracting the disease. Vaccination schedules are determined on a government level and are not optional for pet owners; rabies vaccination is required by law in all 50 states.

Parvovirus: A severe, potentially life-threatening disease that is easily transmitted between dogs. There are four strains of the virus, but it is believed that there is significant "cross-protection" between strains that may be included in individual vaccines.

Distemper: A potentially severe and life-threatening disease with a relatively high risk of exposure, especially in certain regions. In very high-risk distemper environments, young pups may be vaccinated with human measles vaccine, a related virus that offers cross-protection when administered at four to ten weeks of age.

Hepatitis: Caused by canine adenovirus type 1 (CAV-1), but since vaccination with the causative virus has a higher rate of adverse effects, cross-protection is derived from the use of adenovirus type 2 (CAV-2), a cause of respiratory disease and one of the potential causes of canine cough. Vaccination with CAV-2 provides long-term immunity against hepatitis, but relatively less protection against respiratory infection.

Canine cough: Also called tracheobronchitis, actually a fairly complicated result of viral and bacterial offenders; therefore, even with vaccination, protection is incomplete. Wherever dogs congregate, canine cough will likely be spread among them. Intranasal vaccination with *Bordetella* and parainfluenza is the best safeguard, but the duration of immunity does not appear to be very long, typically a year at most. These are non-core vaccines, but vaccination is sometimes mandated by boarding kennels, obedience classes, dog shows and other places where dogs congregate to try to minimize spread of infection.

Leptospirosis: A potentially fatal disease that is more common in some geographic regions. It is capable of being spread to humans. The disease varies with the individual "serovar," or strain, of *Leptospira* involved. Since there does not appear to be much cross-protection between serovars, protection is only as good as the likelihood that the serovar in the vaccine is the same as the one in the pet's local environment. Problems with *Leptospira* vaccines are that protection does not last very long, side effects are not uncommon and a large percentage of dogs (perhaps 30%) may not respond to vaccination.

Borrelia burgdorferi: The cause of Lyme disease, the risk of which varies with the geographic area in which the pet lives and travels. Lyme disease is spread by deer ticks in the eastern US and western black-legged ticks in the western part of the country, and the risk of exposure is high in some regions. Lameness, fever and inappetence are most commonly seen in affected dogs. The extent of protection from the vaccine has not been conclusively demonstrated.

Coronavirus: This disease has a high risk of exposure, especially in areas where dogs congregate, but it typically causes only mild to moderate digestive upset (diarrhea, vomiting, etc.). Vaccines are available, but the duration of protection is believed to be relatively short and the effectiveness of the vaccine in preventing infection is considered low.

There are many other vaccinations available, including those for *Giardia* and canine adenovirus-1. While there may be some specific indications for their use, and local risk factors to be considered, they are not widely recommended for most dogs.

the risk of pet overpopulation, there are also some medical and behavioral benefits to the surgeries as well. For females,

YOUR DOG NEEDS TO VISIT THE VET IF:

• He has ingested a toxin such as antifreeze or a toxic plant; in these cases, administer first aid and call the vet right away;
• His teeth are discolored, loose or missing or he has sores or other signs of infection or abnormality in the mouth;
• He has been vomiting, has had diarrhea or has been constipated for over 24 hours; call immediately if you notice blood;
• He has refused food for over 24 hours;
• His eating habits, water intake or toilet habits have noticeably changed; if you have noticed weight gain or weight loss;
• He shows symptoms of bloat, which requires *immediate* attention;
• He is salivating excessively;
• He has a lump in his throat;
• He has a lump or bumps anywhere on the body;
• He is very lethargic;
• He appears to be in pain or otherwise has trouble chewing or swallowing;
• His skin loses elasticity.

   There will be other instances in which a visit to the vet is necessary; these are just some of the signs that could be indicative of serious problems that need to be caught as early as possible.

spaying prior to the first estrus (heat cycle) leads to a marked reduction in the risk of mammary cancer. There also will be no manifestations of "heat" to attract male dogs and no bleeding in the house. For males, there is prevention of testicular cancer and a reduction in the risk of prostate problems. In both sexes there may be some limited reduction in aggressive behaviors toward other dogs, and some diminishing of urine marking, roaming and mounting.

   While neutering and spaying do indeed prevent animals from contributing to pet overpopulation, even no-cost and low-cost neutering options have not eliminated the problem. Perhaps one of the main reasons for this is that individuals that intentionally breed their dogs and those that allow their animals to run at large are the main causes of unwanted offspring. Also, animals in shelters are often there because they were abandoned or relinquished, not because they came from unplanned matings. Neutering/spaying is important, but it should be considered in the context of the real causes of animals' ending up in shelters and eventually being euthanized.

   One of the important considerations regarding neutering is that it is a surgical procedure. This sometimes gets lost in discussions of low-cost procedures and commoditization of the process. In females, spaying is specifically referred to as an ovariohysterectomy. In this procedure, a midline incision is made in the abdomen and the entire uterus and both ovaries are surgically removed. While this is a major invasive surgical procedure, it usually has few complications, because it is typically performed on healthy young animals. However, it is major surgery, as any woman who has had a hysterectomy will attest.

In males, neutering has traditionally referred to castration, which involves the surgical removal of both testicles. While still a significant piece of surgery, there is not the abdominal exposure that is required in the female surgery. In addition, there is now a chemical sterilization option, in which a solution is injected into each testicle, leading to atrophy of the sperm-producing cells. This can typically be done under sedation rather than full anesthesia. This is a relatively new approach, and there are no long-term clinical studies yet available.

Neutering/spaying is typically done around six months of age at most veterinary hospitals, although techniques have been pioneered to perform the procedures in animals as young as eight weeks of age. In general, the surgeries on the very young animals are done for the specific reason of sterilizing them before

they go to their new homes. This is done in some shelter hospitals for assurance that the animals will definitely not produce any pups. Otherwise, these organizations need to rely on owners to comply with their wishes to have the animals "altered" at a later date, something that does not always happen.

There are some exciting immunocontraceptive "vaccines" currently under development, and there may be a time when contraception in pets will not require surgical procedures. We anxiously await these developments.

Vaccinations are just one of the avenues by which you can attempt to keep your Tervuren free from disease.

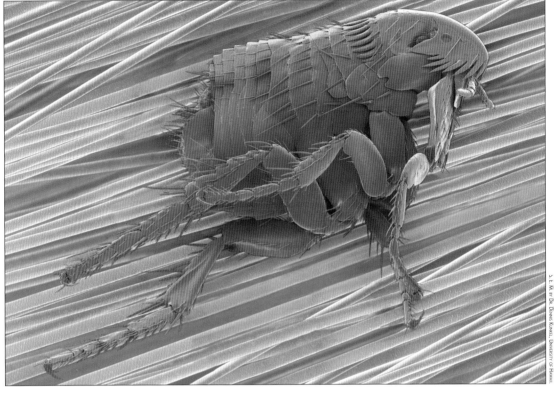

A scanning electron micrograph of a dog flea, *Ctenocephalides canis,* on dog hair.

EXTERNAL PARASITES

FLEAS

Fleas have been around for millions of years and, while we have better tools now for controlling them than at any time in the past, there still is little chance that they will end up on an endangered species list. Actually, they are very well adapted to living on our pets, and they continue to adapt as we make advances.

The female flea can consume 15 times her weight in blood during active reproduction and can lay as many as 40 eggs a day. These eggs are very resistant to the effects of insecticides. They hatch into larvae, which then mature and spin cocoons. The immature fleas reside in this pupal stage until the time is right for feeding. This pupal stage is also very resistant to the effects of insecticides, and pupae can last in the environment without feeding for many months. Newly emergent fleas are attracted to animals by the warmth of the animals' bodies, movement and exhaled carbon dioxide. However, when they first emerge from their cocoons, they orient towards light; thus when an animal passes between a flea and the light source, casting a shadow, the flea pounces and starts to feed. If the animal turns out to be a dog or cat, the reproductive cycle continues. If the flea lands on another type of animal, including a person, the flea will bite but will then look for a more appropriate host. An emerging adult flea can survive without feeding for up to 12 months but, once it tastes blood, it can survive off its host for only 3 to 4 days.

It was once thought that fleas spend most of their lives in the environment, but we now know that fleas won't willingly jump off a dog unless leaping to another dog or when physically removed by brushing, bathing or other manipulation. Flea eggs, on the other hand, are shiny and smooth, and they roll off the animal and into the environment. The eggs, larvae and pupae then exist in the environment, but once the adult finds a susceptible animal, it's home sweet home until the flea is forced to seek refuge elsewhere.

Since adult fleas live on the animal and immature forms survive in the environment, a successful treatment plan must address all stages of the flea life cycle. There are now several safe and effective flea-control products that can be applied on a monthly

FLEA PREVENTION FOR YOUR DOG

- Discuss with your veterinarian the safest product to protect your dog, likely in the form of a monthly tablet or a liquid preparation placed on the back of the dog's neck.
- For dogs suffering from flea-bite dermatitis, a shampoo or topical insecticide treatment is required.
- Your lawn and property should be sprayed with an insecticide designed to kill fleas and ticks that lurk outdoors.
- Using a flea comb, check the dog's coat regularly for any signs of parasites.
- Practice good housekeeping. Vacuum floors, carpets and furniture regularly, especially in the areas that the dog frequents, and wash the dog's bedding weekly.
- Follow up house-cleaning with carpet shampoos and sprays to rid the house of fleas at all stages of development. Insect growth regulators are the safest option.

basis. These include fipronil, imidacloprid, selamectin and permethrin (found in several formulations). Most of these products have significant flea-killing rates within 24 hours. However, none of them will control the immature forms in the environment. To accomplish this, there are a variety of insect growth regulators that can be

THE FLEA'S LIFE CYCLE

What came first, the flea or the egg? This age-old mystery is more difficult to comprehend than the actual cycle of the flea. Fleas usually live only about four months. A female can lay 2,000 eggs in her lifetime.

PHOTO BY CAROLINA BIOLOGICAL SUPPLY CO.

Egg

After ten days of rolling around your carpet or under your furniture, the eggs hatch into larvae, which feed on various and sundry debris. In days or months, depending on the climate, the larvae spin cocoons and develop into the pupal or nymph stage, which quickly develop into fleas.

Larva

PHOTO BY CAROLINA BIOLOGICAL SUPPLY CO.

Pupa

These immature fleas must locate a host within 10 to 14 days or they will die. Only about 1% of the flea population exist as adult fleas, while the other 99% exist as eggs, larvae or pupae.

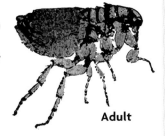

Adult

KILL FLEAS THE NATURAL WAY

If you choose not to go the route of conventional medication, there are some natural ways to ward off fleas:

- Dust your dog with a natural flea powder, composed of such herbal goodies as rosemary, wormwood, pennyroyal, citronella, rue, tobacco powder and eucalyptus.
- Apply diatomaceous earth, the fossilized remains of single-cell algae, to your carpets, furniture and pet's bedding. Even though it's not good for dogs, it's even worse for fleas, which will dry up swiftly and die.
- Brush your dog frequently, give him adequate exercise and let him fast occasionally. All of these activities strengthen the dog's system and make him more resistant to disease and parasites.
- Bathe your dog with a capful of pennyroyal or eucalyptus oil.
- Feed a natural diet, free of additives and preservatives. Add some fresh garlic and brewer's yeast to the dog's morning portion, as these items have flea-repelling properties.

sprayed into the environment (e.g., pyriproxyfen, methoprene, fenoxycarb) as well as insect development inhibitors such as lufenuron that can be administered. These compounds have no effect on adult fleas, but they stop immature forms from developing into adults. In years gone by, we relied heavily on toxic insecticides (such as organophosphates, organochlorines and carbamates) to manage the flea problem, but today's options are not only much safer to use on our pets but also safer for the environment.

TICKS

Ticks are members of the spider class (arachnids) and are blood-sucking parasites capable of transmitting a variety of diseases, including Lyme disease, ehrlichiosis, babesiosis and Rocky Mountain spotted fever. It's easy to see ticks on your own skin, but it is more of a challenge when your furry companion is affected. Whenever you happen to be planning a stroll in a tick-infested area (especially forests, grassy or wooded areas or parks) be prepared to do a thorough inspection of your dog afterward to search for ticks. Ticks can be tricky, so make sure you spend time looking in the ears, between the toes and everywhere else where a tick might hide. Ticks need to be attached for 24–72 hours before they transmit most of the diseases that they carry, so you do have a window of opportunity for some preventive intervention.

A TICKING BOMB

There is nothing good about a tick's harpooning his nose into your dog's skin. Among the diseases caused by ticks are Rocky Mountain spotted fever, canine ehrlichiosis, canine babesiosis, canine hepatozoonosis and Lyme disease. If a dog is allergic to the saliva of a female wood tick, he can develop tick paralysis.

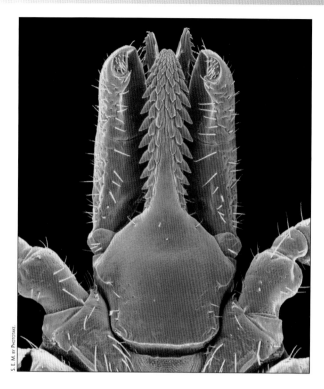

S. E. M. BY PHOTOTAKE.

Female ticks live to eat and breed. They can lay between 4,000 and 5,000 eggs and they die soon after. Males, on the other hand, live only to mate with the females and continue the process as long as they are able. Most ticks live on multiple hosts before parasitizing dogs. The immature forms typically reside on grass and shrubs, waiting for susceptible animals to walk by. The larvae and nymph stages typically feed on wildlife.

If only a few ticks are present on a dog, they can be plucked out, but it is important to remove the entire head and mouthparts,

A scanning electron micrograph of the head of a female deer tick, *Ixodes dammini*, a parasitic tick that carries Lyme disease.

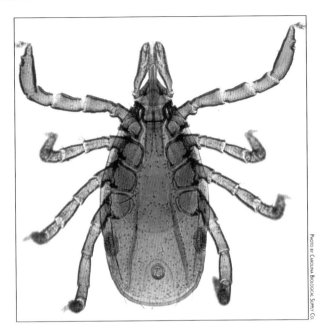

PHOTO BY CAROLINA BIOLOGICAL SUPPLY CO.

Deer tick,
Ixodes dammini.

disposed of in a container of alcohol or household bleach.

Some of the newer flea products, specifically those with fipronil, selamectin and permethrin, have effect against some, but not all, species of tick. Flea collars containing appropriate pesticides (e.g., propoxur, chlorfen-vinphos) can aid in tick control. In most areas, such collars should be placed on animals in March, at the beginning of the tick season, and changed regularly. Leaving the collar on when the pesticide level is waning invites the development of resistance. Amitraz collars are also good for tick control, and the active ingredient does not interfere with other flea-control products. The ingredient helps prevent the attachment of ticks to the skin and will cause those ticks already on the skin to detach themselves.

which may be deeply embedded in the skin. This is best accomplished with forceps designed especially for this purpose; fingers can be used but should be protected with rubber gloves, plastic wrap or at least a paper towel. The tick should be grasped as closely as possible to the animal's skin and should be pulled upward with steady, even pressure. Do not squeeze, crush or puncture the body of the tick or you risk exposure to any disease carried by that tick. Once the ticks have been removed, the sites of attachment should be disinfected. Your hands should then be washed with soap and water to further minimize risk of contagion. The tick should be

TICK CONTROL

Removal of underbrush and leaf litter and the thinning of trees in areas where tick control is desired are recommended. These actions remove the cover and food sources for small animals that serve as hosts for ticks. With continued mowing of grasses in these areas, the probability of ticks' surviving is further reduced. A variety of insecticide ingredients (e.g., resmethrin, carbaryl, permethrin, chlorpyrifos, dioxathion and allethrin) are registered for tick control around the home.

MITES

Mites are tiny arachnid parasites that parasitize the skin of dogs. Skin diseases caused by mites are referred to as "mange," and there are many different forms seen in dogs. These forms are very different from one another, each one warranting an individual description.

Sarcoptic mange, or scabies, is one of the itchiest conditions that affects dogs. The microscopic *Sarcoptes* mites burrow into the superficial layers of the skin and can drive dogs crazy with itchiness. They are also communicable to people, although they can't complete their reproductive cycle on people. In addition to being tiny, the mites also are often difficult to find when trying to make a diagnosis. Skin scrapings from multiple areas are examined microscopically but, even then, sometimes the mites cannot be found.

Fortunately, scabies is relatively easy to treat, and there are a variety of products that will successfully kill the mites. Since the mites can't live in the environment for very long without feeding, a complete cure is usually possible within four to eight weeks.

Cheyletiellosis is caused by a relatively large mite, which sometimes can be seen even without a microscope. Often referred to as "walking dandruff," this also causes itching, but not usually as profound as with scabies. While *Cheyletiella*

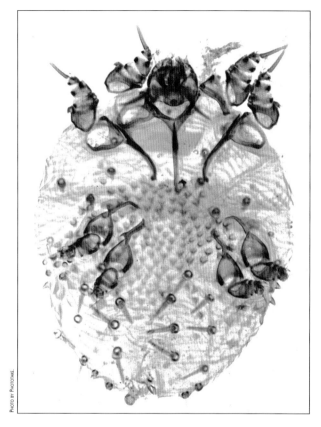

PHOTO BY PHOTOTAKE.

mites can survive somewhat longer in the environment than scabies mites, they too are relatively easy to treat, being responsive to not only the medications used to treat scabies but also often to flea-control products.

Otodectes cynotis is the canine ear mite and is one of the more common causes of mange, especially in young dogs in shelters or pet stores. That's because the mites are typically present in large numbers and are quickly spread to nearby animals. The mites rarely do

Sarcoptes scabiei, commonly known as the "itch mite."

Micrograph of a dog louse, *Heterodoxus spiniger*. Female lice attach their eggs to the hairs of the dog. As the eggs hatch, the larval lice bite and feed on the blood. Lice can also feed on dead skin and hair. This feeding activity can cause hair loss and skin problems.

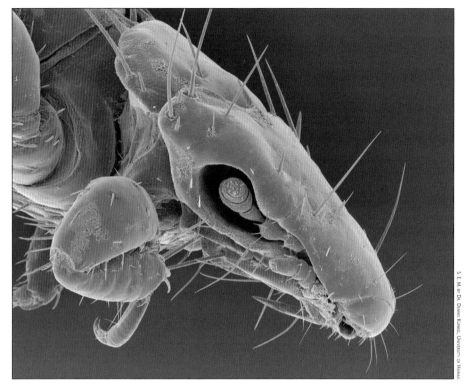

much harm but can be difficult to eradicate if the treatment regimen is not comprehensive. While many try to treat the condition with ear drops only, this is the most common cause of treatment failure. Ear drops cause the mites to simply move out of the ears and as far away as possible (usually to the base of the tail) until the insecticide levels in the ears drop to an acceptable level—then it's back to business as usual! The successful treatment of ear mites requires treating all animals in the household with a systemic insecticide, such as selamectin, or a combination of miticidal ear drops combined with whole-body flea-control preparations.

Demodicosis, sometimes referred to as red mange, can be one of the most difficult forms of mange to treat. Part of the problem has to do with the fact that the mites live in the hair follicles and they are relatively well shielded from topical and systemic products. The main issue, however, is that demodectic mange typically results only when there is some underlying process interfering with the dog's immune system.

Since *Demodex* mites are normal residents of the skin of

mammals, including humans, there is usually a mite population explosion only when the immune system fails to keep the number of mites in check. In young animals, the immune deficit may be transient or may reflect an actual inherited immune problem. In older animals, demodicosis is usually seen only when there is another disease hampering the immune system, such as diabetes, cancer, thyroid problems or the use of immune-suppressing drugs. Accordingly, treatment involves not only trying to kill the mange mites but also discerning what is interfering with immune function and correcting it if possible.

Chiggers represent several different species of mite that don't parasitize dogs specifically, but do latch on to passersby and can cause irritation. The problem is most prevalent in wooded areas in the late summer and fall. Treatment is not difficult, as the mites do not complete their life cycle on dogs and are susceptible to a variety of miticidal products.

MOSQUITOES

Mosquitoes have long been known to transmit a variety of diseases to people, as well as just being biting pests during warm weather. They also pose a real risk to pets. Not only do they carry deadly heartworms but

recently there also has been much concern over their involvement with West Nile virus. While we can avoid heartworm with the use of preventive medications, there are no such preventives for West Nile virus. The only method of prevention in endemic areas is active mosquito control. Fortunately, most dogs that have been exposed to the virus only developed flu-like symptoms and, to date, there have not been the large number of reported deaths in canines as seen in some other species.

Illustration of Demodex folliculoram.

MOSQUITO REPELLENT

Low concentrations of DEET (less than 10%), found in many human mosquito repellents, have been safely used in dogs but, in these concentrations, probably give only about two hours of protection. DEET may be safe in these small concentrations, but since it is not licensed for use on dogs, there is no research proving its safety for dogs. Products containing permethrin give the longest-lasting protection, perhaps two to four weeks. As DEET is not licensed for use on dogs, and both DEET and permethrin can be quite toxic to cats, appropriate care should be exercised. Other products, such as those containing oil of citronella, also have some mosquito-repellent activity, but typically have a relatively short duration of action.

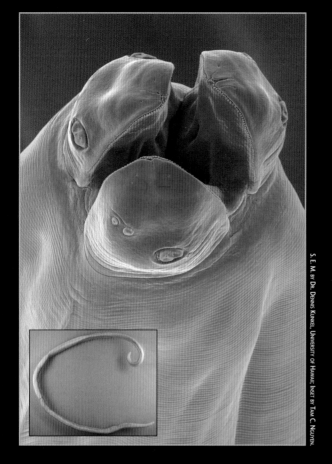

The ascarid roundworm *Toxocara canis,* showing the mouth with three lips. INSET: Photomicrograph of the roundworm *Ascaris lumbricoides.*

S. E. M. BY DR. DENNIS KUNKEL, UNIVERSITY OF HAWAII; INSET BY TAM C. NGUYEN.

INTERNAL PARASITES: WORMS

ASCARIDS

Ascarids are intestinal roundworms that rarely cause severe disease in dogs. Nonetheless, they are of major public health significance because they can be transferred to people. Sadly, it is children who are most commonly affected by the parasite, probably from inadvertently ingesting ascarid-contaminated soil. In fact, many yards and children's sandboxes contain appreciable numbers of ascarid eggs. So, while ascarids don't bite dogs or latch onto their intestines to suck blood, they do cause some nasty medical conditions in children and are best eradicated from our furry friends. Because pups can start passing ascarid eggs by three weeks of age, most parasite-control programs begin at two weeks of age and are repeated every two weeks until pups are eight weeks old. It is

HOOKED ON ANCYLOSTOMA

Adult dogs can become infected by the bloodsucking nematodes we commonly call hookworms via ingesting larvae from the ground or via the larvae penetrating the dog's skin. It is not uncommon for infected dogs to show no symptoms of hookworm infestation. Sometimes symptoms occur within ten days of exposure. These symptoms can include bloody diarrhea, anemia, loss of weight and general weakness. Dogs pass the hookworm eggs in their stools, which serves as the vet's method of identi-fying the infestation. The hookworm larvae can encyst themselves in the dog's tissues and be released when the dog is experiencing stress.

Caused by an *Ancylostoma* species whose common host is the dog, cutaneous larval migrans affects humans, causing itching and lumps and streaks beneath the surface of the skin.

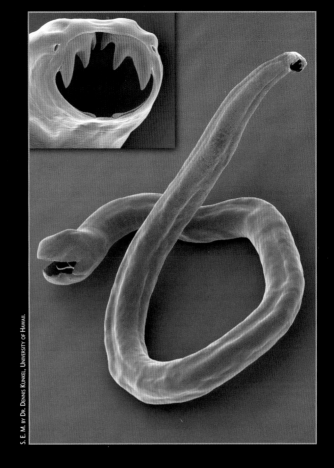

important to realize that bitches can pass ascarids to their pups even if they test negative prior to whelping. Accordingly, bitches are best treated at the same time as the pups.

HOOKWORMS

Unlike ascarids, hookworms do latch onto a dog's intestinal tract and can cause significant loss of blood and protein. Similar to ascarids, hookworms can be transmitted to humans, where they cause a condition known as cutaneous larval migrans. Dogs can become infected either by consuming the infective larvae or by the larvae's penetrating the skin directly. People most often get infected when they are lying on the ground (such as on a beach) and the larvae penetrate the skin. Yes, the larvae can penetrate through a beach blanket. Hookworms are typically suscep-tible to the same medications used to treat ascarids.

The hookworm *Ancylostoma caninum* infests the intestines of dogs. INSET: Note the row of hooks at the posterior end, used to anchor the worm to the intestinal wall.

WHIPWORMS

Whipworms latch onto the lower aspects of the dog's colon and can cause cramping and diarrhea. Eggs do not start to appear in the dog's feces until about three months after the dog was infected. This worm has a peculiar life cycle, which makes it more difficult to control than ascarids or hookworms. The good thing is that whipworms rarely are transferred to people.

Some of the medications used to treat ascarids and hookworms are also effective against whipworms, but, in general, a separate treatment protocol is needed. Since most of the medications are effective against the adults but not the eggs or larvae, treatment is typically repeated in three weeks, and then often in three

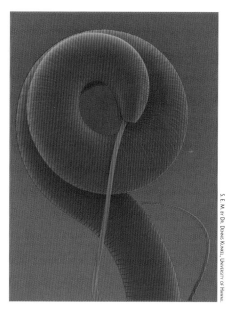

Adult whipworm, *Trichuris* sp., an intestinal parasite.

S. E. M. BY DR. DENNIS KUNKEL, UNIVERSITY OF HAWAII

WORM-CONTROL GUIDELINES

- Practice sanitary habits with your dog and home.
- Clean up after your dog and don't let him sniff or eat other dogs' droppings.
- Control insects and fleas in the dog's environment. Fleas, lice, cockroaches, beetles, mice and rats can act as hosts for various worms.
- Prevent dogs from eating uncooked meat, raw poultry and dead animals.
- Keep dogs and children from playing in sand and soil.
- Kennel dogs on cement or gravel; avoid dirt runs.
- Administer heartworm preventives regularly.
- Have your vet examine your dog's stools at your annual visits.
- Select a boarding kennel carefully so as to avoid contamination from other dogs or an unsanitary environment.
- Prevent dogs from roaming. Obey local leash laws.

months as well. Unfortunately, since dogs don't develop resistance to whipworms, it is difficult to prevent them from getting reinfected if they visit soil contaminated with whipworm eggs.

TAPEWORMS

There are many different species of tapeworm that affect dogs, but *Dipylidium caninum* is probably the most common and is spread by fleas. Flea larvae feed on organic debris and tapeworm eggs in the environment and, when a dog chews at himself and manages to ingest fleas, he might get a dose of tapeworm at the same time. The tapeworm then develops further in the intestine of the dog.

The tapeworm itself, which is a parasitic flatworm that latches onto the intestinal wall, is composed of numerous segments. When the segments break off into the intestine (as proglottids), they may accumulate around the rectum, like grains of rice. While this tapeworm is disgusting in its behavior, it is not directly communicable to humans (although humans can also get infected by swallowing fleas).

A much more dangerous tapeworm is *Echinococcus multilocularis*, which is typically found in foxes, coyotes and wolves. The eggs are passed in the feces and infect rodents, and, when dogs eat the rodents, the dogs can be infected by thousands of adult tapeworms. While the parasites don't cause many problems in dogs, this is considered the most lethal worm infection that people can get. Take appropriate precautions if you live in an area in which these tapeworms are found. Do not use mulch that may contain feces of dogs, cats or wildlife, and

discourage your pets from hunting wildlife. Treat these tapeworm infections aggressively in pets, because if humans get infected, approximately half die.

HEARTWORMS

Heartworm disease is caused by the parasite *Dirofilaria immitis* and is seen in dogs around the world. A member of the roundworm group, it is spread between dogs by the bite of an infected mosquito. The mosquito injects infective larvae into the dog's skin with its bite, and these larvae develop under the skin for a period of time before making their way to the heart. There they develop into adults, which grow and create blockages of the heart, lungs and major blood vessels there. They also start producing offspring (microfilariae),

A dog tapeworm proglottid (body segment).

The dog tapeworm *Taenia pisiformis*.

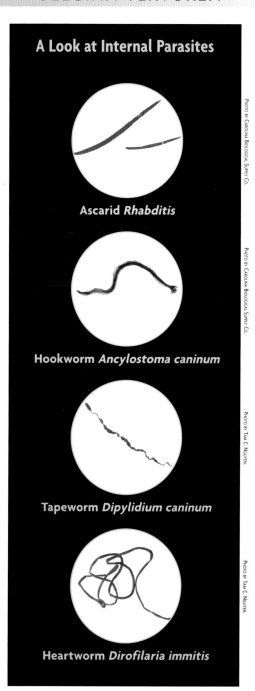

A Look at Internal Parasites

Ascarid *Rhabditis*

Hookworm *Ancylostoma caninum*

Tapeworm *Dipylidium caninum*

Heartworm *Dirofilaria immitis*

PHOTO BY CAROLINA BIOLOGICAL SUPPLY CO.

PHOTO BY CAROLINA BIOLOGICAL SUPPLY CO.

PHOTO BY TAM C NGUYEN.

PHOTO BY TAM C NGUYEN.

and these microfilariae circulate in the bloodstream, waiting to hitch a ride when the next mosquito bites. Once in the mosquito, the microfilariae develop into infective larvae and the entire process is repeated.

When dogs get infected with heartworm, over time they tend to develop symptoms associated with heart disease, such as coughing, exercise intolerance and potentially many other manifestations. Diagnosis is confirmed by either seeing the microfilariae themselves in blood samples or using immunologic tests (antigen testing) to identify the presence of adult heartworms. Since antigen tests measure the presence of adult heartworms and microfilarial tests measure offspring produced by adults, neither are positive until six to seven months after the initial infection. However, the beginning of damage can occur by fifth-stage larvae as early as three months after infection. Thus it is possible for dogs to be harboring problem-causing larvae for up to three months before either type of test would identify an infection.

The good news is that there are great protocols available for preventing heartworm in dogs. Testing is critical in the process, and it is important to understand the benefits as well as the limitations of such testing. All dogs six months of age or older that have not been on continuous heartworm-preventive medication should be

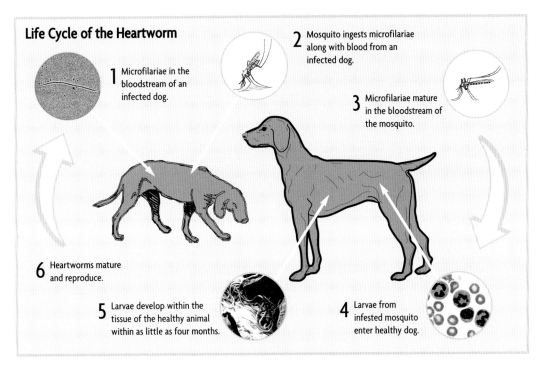

Life Cycle of the Heartworm

1 Microfilariae in the bloodstream of an infected dog.

2 Mosquito ingests microfilariae along with blood from an infected dog.

3 Microfilariae mature in the bloodstream of the mosquito.

4 Larvae from infested mosquito enter healthy dog.

5 Larvae develop within the tissue of the healthy animal within as little as four months.

6 Heartworms mature and reproduce.

screened with microfilarial or antigen tests. For dogs receiving preventive medication, periodic antigen testing helps assess the effectiveness of the preventives. The American Heartworm Society guidelines suggest that annual retesting may not be necessary when owners have absolutely provided continuous heartworm prevention. Retesting on a two- to three-year interval may be sufficient in these cases. However, your veterinarian will likely have specific guidelines under which heartworm preventives will be prescribed, and many prefer to err on the side of safety and retest annually.

It is indeed fortunate that heartworm is relatively easy to prevent, because treatments can be as life-threatening as the disease itself. Treatment requires a two-step process that kills the adult heartworms first and then the microfilariae. Prevention is obviously preferable; this involves a once-monthly oral or topical treatment. The most common oral preventives include ivermectin (not suitable for some breeds), moxidectin and milbemycin oxime; the once-a-month topical drug selamectin provides heartworm protection in addition to flea, some types of tick and other parasite controls.

THE **ABC**s OF
Emergency Care

Abrasions
Clean wound with running water or 3% hydrogen peroxide. Pat dry with gauze and spray with antibiotic. Do not cover.

Animal Bites
Clean area with soap and saline solution or water. Apply pressure to any bleeding area. Apply antibiotic ointment. Identify biting animal and contact the vet.

Antifreeze Poisoning
Induce vomiting and take dog to the vet.

Bee Sting
Remove stinger and apply soothing lotion or cold compress; give antihistamine in proper dosage.

Bleeding
Apply pressure directly to wound with gauze or towel for five to ten minutes. If wound does not stop bleeding, wrap wound with gauze and adhesive tape.

Bloat/Gastric Torsion
Immediately take the dog to the vet or emergency clinic; phone from car. No time to waste.

Burns
Chemical: Bathe dog with water and pet shampoo. Rinse in saline solution. Apply antibiotic ointment.

Acid: Rinse with water. Apply one part baking soda, two parts water to affected area.

Alkali: Rinse with water. Apply one part vinegar, four parts water to affected area.

Electrical: Apply antibiotic ointment. Seek veterinary assistance immediately.

Choking
If the dog is on the verge of collapsing, wedge a solid object, such as the handle of a screwdriver, between molars on one side of mouth to keep mouth open. Pull tongue out. Use long-nosed pliers or fingers to remove foreign object. Do not push the object down the dog's throat. For small or medium dogs, hold dog upside down by hind legs and shake firmly to dislodge foreign object.

Chlorine Ingestion
With clean water, rinse the mouth and eyes. Give dog water to drink; contact the vet.

Constipation
Feed dog 2 tablespoons bran flakes with each meal. Encourage drinking water. Mix 1/4-teaspoon mineral oil in dog's food. Contact vet if persists longer than 24 hours.

Diarrhea
Withhold food for 12 to 24 hours. Feed dog antidiarrheal with eyedropper. When feeding resumes, feed one part boiled hamburger, one part plain cooked rice, 1/4 to 3/4 cup four times daily. Contact vet if persists longer than 24 hours.

Dog Bite
Snip away hair around puncture wound; clean with 3% hydrogen peroxide; apply tincture of iodine. Identify biting dog and call the vet. If wound appears deep, take the dog to the vet.

Frostbite
Wrap the dog in a heavy blanket. Warm affected area with a warm bath for ten minutes. Red color to skin will return with circulation; if tissues are pale after 20 minutes, contact the vet.

Use a portable, durable container large enough to contain all items.

Heat Stroke
Submerge the dog (up to his muzzle) in cold water; if no response within ten minutes, contact the vet.

Hot Spots
Mix 2 packets Domeboro® with 2 cups water. Saturate cloth with mixture and apply to hot spots for 15–30 minutes. Apply antibiotic ointment. Repeat every six to eight hours.

Poisonous Plants
Wash affected area with soap and water. Cleanse with alcohol. For foxtail/grass, apply antibiotic ointment. Contact vet if plant was ingested.

Rat Poison Ingestion
Induce vomiting. Keep dog calm, maintain dog's normal body temperature (use blanket or heating pad). Get to the vet for antidote.

Shock
Keep the dog calm and warm; call for veterinary assistance.

Snake Bite
If possible, bandage the area and apply pressure. If the area is not conducive to bandaging, use ice to control bleeding. Get immediate help from the vet.

Tick Removal
Apply flea and tick spray directly on tick. Wait one minute. Using tweezers or wearing plastic gloves, grasp the tick's body firmly and pull out. Apply antibiotic ointment.

Vomiting
Restrict water intake; offer a few ice cubes. Withhold food for next meal. Contact vet if vomiting persists longer than 24 hours.

DOG OWNER'S FIRST-AID KIT
- ❑ Gauze bandages/swabs
- ❑ Adhesive and non-adhesive bandages
- ❑ Antibiotic powder
- ❑ Antiseptic wash
- ❑ Hydrogen peroxide 3%
- ❑ Antibiotic ointment
- ❑ Lubricating jelly
- ❑ Rectal thermometer
- ❑ Nylon muzzle
- ❑ Scissors and forceps
- ❑ Eyedropper
- ❑ Syringe
- ❑ Anti-bacterial/fungal solution
- ❑ Saline solution
- ❑ Antihistamine
- ❑ Cotton balls
- ❑ Nail clippers
- ❑ Screwdriver/pen knife
- ❑ Flashlight
- ❑ Emergency phone numbers

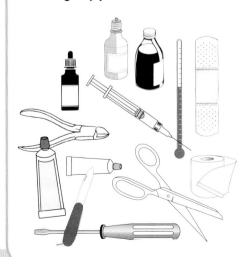

SHOWING YOUR

BELGIAN TERVUREN

Is dog showing in your blood? Are you excited by the idea of gaiting your handsome Belgian Tervuren around the ring to the thunderous applause of an enthusiastic audience? Are you certain that your beloved Belgian Tervuren is flawless? You are not alone! Every loving owner thinks that his dog has no faults, or too few to mention. No matter how many times an owner reads the breed standard, he cannot find any faults in his aristocratic companion dog. If this sounds like you, and if you are considering entering your Belgian Tervuren in a dog show, here are some basic questions to ask yourself:

- Did you purchase a "show-quality" puppy from the breeder?
- Is your puppy at least six months of age?
- Does the puppy exhibit correct show type for his breed?
- Does your puppy have any disqualifying faults?
- Is your Belgian Tervuren registered with the American Kennel Club?
- How much time do you have to devote to training, grooming, conditioning and exhibiting your dog?
- Do you understand the rules and regulations of a dog show?
- Do you have time to learn how to show your dog properly?
- Do you have the financial resources to invest in showing your dog?
- Will you show the dog yourself or hire a professional handler?
- Do you have a vehicle that can accommodate your weekend trips to the dog shows?

Success in the show ring requires more than a pretty face, a waggy tail and a pocketful of liver. Even though dog shows can be exciting and enjoyable, the sport of conformation makes great demands on the exhibitors and the dogs. Winning exhibitors live for their dogs, devoting time and money to their dogs' presentation, conditioning and training. Very few novices, even those with good dogs,

AKC GROUPS

For showing purposes, the American Kennel Club divides its recognized breeds into seven groups: Herding Dogs, Sporting Dogs, Hounds, Working Dogs, Terriers, Toys and Non-Sporting Dogs.

will find themselves in the winners' circle, though it does happen. Don't be disheartened, though. Every exhibitor began as a novice and worked his way up to the group ring. It's the "working your way up" part that you must keep in mind.

Assuming that you have purchased a puppy of the correct type and quality for showing, let's begin to examine the world of showing and what's required to get started. Although the entry fee into a dog show is nominal, there are lots of other hidden costs involved with "finishing" your Belgian Tervuren, that is, making him a champion. Things like equipment, travel, training and conditioning all cost money. A more serious campaign will include fees for a professional handler, boarding, cross-country travel and advertising. Top-winning show dogs can represent a very considerable investment—over $100,000 has been spent in campaigning some dogs. (The investment can be less, of course, for owners who don't use professional handlers.)

Many owners, on the other hand, enter their "average" Belgian Tervuren in dog shows for the fun and enjoyment of it. Dog showing makes an absorbing hobby, with many rewards for dogs and owners alike. If you're having fun, meeting other people who share your interests and enjoying the overall experience, you likely will catch

the "bug." Once the dog-show bug bites, its effects can last a lifetime; it's certainly much better than a deer tick! Soon you will be envisioning yourself in the center ring at the Westminster Kennel Club Dog Show in New York City, competing for the prestigious Best in Show cup. This magical dog show is televised annually from Madison Square Garden, and the victorious dog becomes a celebrity overnight.

At Westminster Kennel Club in 2001 judge Lester Mapes selected Ch. Cinema I Have A Dream CDX, TD, owned by Maureen Foley, as Best of Breed.

AKC CONFORMATION SHOWING

GETTING STARTED

Visiting a dog show as a spectator is a great place to start. Pick up the show catalog to find out what time your breed is being shown, who is judging the breed and in which ring the classes will be held. To start, Belgian Tervurens compete against other Belgian Tervurens, and the winner is selected as Best of Breed by the judge. This is the procedure for each breed. At a group show, all of the Best of Breed winners go on to compete for Group One (first place) in their respective groups. For example, all Best of Breed winners from the Herding Group compete against each other; this is done for all seven groups. Finally, all seven group winners go head to head in the ring for the Best in Show award.

What most spectators don't understand is the basic idea of conformation. A dog show is often referred to as a "conformation" show. This means that the judge should decide how each

dog stacks up (conforms) to the breed standard for his given breed: how well does this Belgian Tervuren conform to the ideal representative detailed in the standard? Ideally, this is what happens. In reality, however, this ideal often gets slighted as the judge compares Belgian Tervuren #1 to Belgian Tervuren #2. Again, the ideal is that each dog is judged based on his merits in comparison to his breed standard, not in comparison to the other dogs in the ring. It is easier for judges to compare dogs of the same breed to decide which they think is the better specimen; in the group and Best in Show ring, however, it is very difficult to compare one breed to another, like apples to oranges. Thus the dog's conformation to the breed standard—not to mention advertising dollars and good handling—is essential to success in conformation shows. The dog described in the standard is the perfect dog of that breed, and breeders keep their eye on the standard when they choose which dogs to breed, hoping to get closer and closer to the ideal with each litter.

Another good first step for the novice is to join a dog club. You will be astonished by the many and different kinds of dog clubs in the country, with about 5,000 clubs holding events every year. Most clubs require that prospec-

The top winning Tervuren for 2003, 2004 and 2005, Ch. Magic's Ty Won On At Char-Ma, shown taking one of his Best in Show wins at Sussex Hills Kennel Club in 2004 under judge Virginia Hampton, handled by Jane Hobson. Owners Frank and Charlene Mascuch.

tive new members present two letters of recommendation from existing members. Perhaps you've made some friends visiting a show held by a particular club and you would like to join that club. Dog clubs may specialize in a single breed, like a regional Belgian Tervuren club, or in a specific pursuit, such as obedience, tracking or herding tests. There are all-breed clubs for all dog enthusiasts; they sponsor special training days, seminars on topics like grooming or handling or lectures on breeding or canine genetics. There are also clubs that specialize in certain types of dogs, like herding dogs, hunting dogs, companion dogs, etc.

A parent club is the national organization, sanctioned by the AKC, which promotes and safeguards its breed in the country. The American Belgian Tervuren Club can be contacted on the Internet at www.abtc.org. The parent club holds an annual national specialty show, in which many of the country's top dogs, handlers and breeders gather to compete. At a specialty show, only members of a single breed are invited to participate. There are also group specialties, in which all members of a group are invited.

How Shows Are Organized

Three kinds of conformation shows are offered by the AKC. There is the all-breed show, in which all AKC-

> **MEET THE AKC**
> The American Kennel Club is the main governing body of the dog sport in the United States. Founded in 1884, the AKC consists of 500 or more independent dog clubs plus 4,500 affiliated clubs, all of which follow the AKC rules and regulations. Additionally, the AKC maintains a registry for purebred dogs in the US and works to preserve the integrity of the sport and its continuation in the country. Over 1,000,000 dogs are registered each year, representing about 150 recognized breeds. There are over 15,000 competitive events held annually for which over 2,000,000 dogs enter to participate. Dogs compete to earn over 40 different titles, from Champion to Companion Dog to Master Agility Champion.

recognized breeds can compete, the specialty show, which is for one breed only and usually sponsored by the breed's parent club and the group show, for all breeds in one of the AKC's seven groups. The Belgian Tervuren competes in the Herding Group.

For a dog to become an AKC champion of record, the dog must earn 15 points at shows. The points must be awarded by at least three different judges and must include two "majors" under different judges. A "major" is a three-, four- or five-point win, and the number of points per win is

Best in Show at
Klamath Dog
Fanciers in 2005
under judge
Robert Lopaschuk
was Ch. Sky Acres
Piper Aerostar,
owned by M.
Edling.

Best in Show at Klamath Dog Fanciers in 2005 under judge Robert Lopaschuk was Ch. Sky Acres Piper Aerostar, owned by M. Edling.

determined by the number of dogs competing in the show on that day. (Dogs that are absent or are excused are not counted.) The number of points that are awarded varies from breed to breed. More dogs are needed to attain a major in more popular breeds, and fewer dogs are needed in less popular breeds. Yearly, the AKC evaluates the number of dogs in competition in each division (there are 14 divisions in all, based on geography) and may or may not change the numbers of dogs required for each number of points. The Belgian Tervuren is entered in relatively small numbers at all-breed shows.

Only one dog and one bitch of each breed can win points at a given show. There are no "co-ed" classes except for champions of record and Winners. Dogs and bitches do not compete against each other until they are champions. Dogs that are not champions (referred to as "class dogs") compete in one of five classes. The class in which a dog is entered depends on age and previous show wins. First there is the Puppy Class (sometimes divided further into classes for 6-

to 9-month-olds and 9- to 12-month-olds); next is the Novice Class (for dogs that have no points toward their championship and whose only first-place wins have come in the Puppy Class or the Novice Class, the latter class limited to 3 first places); then there is the American-bred Class (for dogs bred in the US); next is the Bred-by-Exhibitor Class (for dogs handled by their breeders or by immediate family members of their breeders); and finally, the Open Class (for any non-champions). Any dog may enter the Open Class, regardless of age or win history, but to be competitive the dog should be older and have ring experience.

The judge at the show begins judging the male dogs in the Puppy Class(es) and proceeds through the other classes. The judge awards first through fourth place in each class. The first-place winners of each class then compete with one another in the Winners Class to determine Winners Dog. The judge then starts over with the bitches, beginning with the Puppy Class(es) and proceeding up to the Winners Class to award Winners Bitch, just as he did with the dogs. A Reserve Winners Dog and Reserve Winners Bitch are also selected; they could be awarded the points in the case of a disqualification.

The Winners Dog and Winners Bitch are the two that are awarded the points for their breed. They then go on to compete with any champions of record (often called "specials") of their breed that are entered in the show. The champions may be dogs or bitches; in this class, all are shown together. The judge reviews the Winners Dog and Winners Bitch along with all of the champions to select the Best of Breed winner. The Best of Winners is selected between the Winners Dog and Winners Bitch; if one of these two is selected Best of Breed as well, he or she is automatically determined Best of Winners. Lastly, the judge selects Best of Opposite Sex to the Best of

Attending an outdoor all-breed or specialty show can be an exciting experience for newcomers. You will learn much about how shows work and also more about the Belgian Tervuren.

against one another for Group One through Group Four. Group One (first place) is awarded to the dog that best lives up to the ideal for his breed as described in the standard. A group judge, therefore, must have a thorough working knowledge of many breed standards. After placements have been made in each group, the seven Group One winners compete against each other for the top honor, Best in Show.

OTHER TYPES OF COMPETITION

In addition to conformation shows, the AKC holds a variety of other competitive events. Additionally, the Junior Showmanship program is offered to aspiring young handlers and their dogs, and the Canine Good Citizen® program is an all-around good-behavior test open to all dogs, pure-bred and mixed.

There is little this dynamic, athletic dog can't do, including flying through a tire jump (ABOVE) or firing through the weave poles (BELOW).

Breed winner. The Best of Breed winner then goes on to the group competition.

At a group or all-breed show, the Best of Breed winners from each breed are divided into their respective groups to compete

OBEDIENCE TRIALS

There are three levels of difficulty in obedience competition. The first (and easiest) level is the Novice, in which dogs can earn the Companion Dog (CD) title. The intermediate level is the Open level, in which the Companion Dog Excellent (CDX) title is awarded. The advanced level is the Utility level, in which dogs compete for the Utility Dog (UD) title. Classes at each level are further divided into "A" and "B,"

with "A" for beginners and "B" for those with more experience. In order to win a title at a given level, a dog must earn three "legs." A "leg" is accomplished when a dog scores 170 or higher (200 is a perfect score). The scoring system gets a little trickier when you understand that a dog must score more than 50% of the points available for each exercise in order to actually earn the points. Available points for each exercise range between 20 and 40.

A dog must complete different exercises at each level of obedience. The Novice exercises are the easiest, with the Open and finally the Utility levels progressing in difficulty. Examples of Novice exercises are on- and off-lead heeling, a figure-8 pattern, performing a recall (or come), long

sit and long down and standing for examination. In the Open level, the Novice-level exercises are required again, but this time without a leash and for longer durations. In addition, the dog must clear a broad jump, retrieve over a jump

Whether he is jumping bars with ease (ABOVE) or attacking the tunnel with gusto (BELOW), watching the Belgian in action on the agility course is nearly as exciting as participating.

and drop on recall. In the Utility level, the exercises are quite difficult, including executing basic commands based on hand signals, following a complex heeling pattern, scent discrimination and completing jumps at the handler's direction.

Once he's earned the UD title, a dog can go on to win the prestigious title of Utility Dog Excellent (UDX) by winning "legs" in ten shows. Additionally, Utility Dogs who win "legs" in Open B and Utility B earn points toward the lofty title of Obedience Trial Champion (OTCh.).

AGILITY TRIALS

Agility trials became sanctioned by the AKC in August 1994, when the first licensed agility trials were held. Since that time, agility certainly has grown in popularity by leaps and bounds, literally! The AKC allows all registered breeds (including Miscellaneous Class breeds) to participate, providing the dog is 12 months of age or older. Agility is designed so that the handler demonstrates how well the dog can work at his side. The handler directs his dog through, over, under and around an obstacle course that includes jumps, tires, the dog walk, weave poles, pipe tunnels, collapsed tunnels and more. The handler runs along with the dog, giving verbal and hand signals to guide the dog through the course.

The first organization to promote agility trials in the US was the United States Dog Agility Association, Inc. (USDAA). Established in 1986, the USDAA sparked the formation of many member clubs around the country. To participate in USDAA trials, dogs must be at least 18 months of age.

The USDAA and AKC both offer titles to winning dogs, although the exercises and requirements of the two organizations differ. Agility Dog (AD), Advanced Agility Dog (AAD) and Master Agility Dog (MAD) are the titles offered by the USDAA, while the AKC offers Novice Agility (NA), Open Agility (OA), Agility Excellent (AX) and Master Agility Excellent (MX). Beyond these four AKC titles, dogs can win additional titles in "jumper" classes: Jumper with Weave Novice (NAJ), Open (OAJ) and Excellent (MXJ). The ultimate title in AKC agility is MACH, Master Agility Champion. Dogs can continue to add number designations to the MACH title, indicating how many times the dog has met the title's requirements (MACH1, MACH2 and so on).

TRACKING

Tracking tests are exciting ways to test your Belgian Tervuren's instinctive scenting ability on a competitive level. The Tracking

Dog (TD) level is the first and most basic level in tracking, progressing in difficulty to the Tracking Dog Excellent (TDX) and then the Variable Surface Tracking (VST). A dog must follow a track laid by a human 30 to 120 minutes prior in order to earn the TD title. The track is about 500 yards long and contains up to 5 directional changes. At the next level, the TDX, the dog must follow a 3- to 5-hour-old track over a course that is up to 1,000 yards long and has up to 7 directional changes. In the most difficult level, the VST, the track is up to five hours old and located in an urban setting.

HERDING EVENTS

The first recorded sheepdog trial was held in Wales in the late 19th century; since then, the popularity of herding events has grown around the world. The AKC began offering herding events in 1989, and participation is open to all breeds in the Herding Group as well as Rottweilers and Samoyeds. These events are designed to evaluate the dogs' herding instincts, and the aim is to develop these innate skills and show that herding dogs today can still perform the functions for which they were originally intended, whether or not they are actually used in working capacities. Herding events are designed to simulate

> **RENAISSANCE DOGS**
> Tervurens have done very well in the various areas of working dogs. A notable dog from the 1980s is Kyan Without Wings of Minka, who was cast in a number of movies, appeared in three agility finals and added the following titles to his name: Companion Dog Excellent (CDX), Working Dog Excellent (WDX) and Police Dog Excellent (PDX). Half-sister Kyan Vision of Minka also appeared in films, and Minack Edgemont Chancer, from the same kennel, appeared in the very popular English soap opera *Eastenders* and in the movies *101 Dalmatians* and *102 Dalmatians*. Her offspring have done very well in agility, obedience and working trials.

farm situations and are held on two levels: tests and trials.

AKC herding tests are more basic and are scored on a pass/fail system, meaning that dogs do not compete against each other to earn titles. Titles at this level are the most basic Herding Tested (HT) and the more difficult Pre-Trial Tested (PT). In addition, there is a non-competitive certification program, Herding Instinct Tested, which gives you a chance to evaluate the potential that your dog may have for herding. If your dog successfully passes this test, he receives a Herding Instinct Certificate, which makes him eligible to enter herding trials.

The longhaired Belgian Tervuren negotiating the weave poles is true poetry in motion.

The more challenging herding trial level is competitive and requires more training and experience. There are three different courses (A, B and C, each with a different type of farm situation) with different types of livestock (cattle, sheep or ducks). There are three titles available on each course, Herding Started, Herding Intermediate and Herding Advanced, with each level being progressively more difficult. Handlers can choose the type of course and type of livestock for their dogs based on the breed's typical use. Once a Herding Advanced title has been earned on a course, the dog can then begin to strive for the Herding Champion title.

"What's next?" This Tervuren eagerly looks to the next obstacle at an agility event.

In addition to events held by the AKC, breed clubs often hold herding events for these breeds. Other specialty organizations hold trials that are open to all herding breeds; the way these events are structured and the titles that are awarded differ from those of the AKC. For example, the American Herding Breed Association (AHBA) allows any breed with herding in its ancestry to participate, as well as allowing mixed-breed herding dogs. To pass the Herding Instinct Test, the handler works with the dog at the shepherd's direction while the shepherd evaluates the dog's willingness to approach, move and round up the sheep while at the same time following the instructions of his handler.

At the competition level in AHBA events, dogs work with their handlers to move sheep up and down the field, through gates and into a pen and also to hold the sheep without a pen, all while being timed. This is an amazing sight to see! A good dog working with the shepherd has to be the ultimate man-dog interaction. Rare breeds were often traditionally used for herding and, fortunately, the AHBA is more than happy to have rare breeds participate. Club members and spectators love to welcome some of these wonderful dogs that they have only read about but never seen.

Simulating actual farm work, a herding trial requires the dog to pen the livestock, in this case sheep.

INDEX

My Belgian Tervuren

PUT YOUR PUPPY'S FIRST PICTURE HERE

Dog's Name _____

Date _____ Photographer _____